THE ESSENTIAL TRUTHS OF TRADING

THE ESSENTIAL TRUTHS OF TRADING

The Order Beneath the Chaos

ROWAN QUILL

THE ESSENTIAL TRUTHS OF TRADING

The Order Beneath the Chaos

Rowan Quill is a pen name. Correspondence may be directed through essentialtruthsoftrading.com.

First edition, 2026.

Paperback ISBN 978-1-7648145-0-8

Hardcover ISBN 978-1-7648145-1-5

essentialtruthsoftrading.com

CONTENTS

Preface: Why Truths, Not Laws vii

How to Read This Book ix

The Twelve Truths xi

A Note on Risk xv

PART I · PERCEPTION 1

1 Order 2

2 Objectivity 15

A First Reading · The Same Morning, Twice 26

PART II · ORIENTATION 29

3 Location 30

4 Value 47

5 Time 60

6 Language 72

A Second Reading · The Sweep They Both Saw 85

PART III · EXECUTION 89

7 Framing 90

8 Measurement 103

9 Invalidation 117

A Third Reading · The Trade They Only Seemed to Share 131

PART IV · CONTINUITY 135

10 Repetition 136

11 Process 147

A Fourth Reading · The Leg That Stopped Behaving Like Itself 158

12 Psychology 161

A Fifth Reading · The Trade That Died on Schedule 173

Coda: The Essential Truth 175

Appendix: The Sequence, Stated 178

Afterword: On What Comes After 183

A Glossary of Terms 184

Attributions, Notes and Sources 186

About the Author 188

PREFACE

WHY TRUTHS, NOT LAWS

I HAVE SPENT MOST of my working life in rooms where sequence decides outcomes. In training halls, first: years of them, as an athlete at the top of a sport and then on the coaching floor, where I learned the lesson that eventually became the last chapter of this book, that champions are not found, and are not born, but are assembled, in order, one correctly graded exposure at a time, and that the surest way to destroy a gifted athlete is to give him the right challenges in the wrong sequence. Then in courtrooms and around negotiating tables, where the same law wears a wig: cases are won by the order in which evidence is laid, and I watched strong claims die because they were pleaded vaguely and weak ones survive because they were framed with precision. Business taught the same law at company scale: I have founded companies, run an investment firm, and patented inventions, and every venture that worked was a sequence before it was a success, while every one that struggled had skipped a step that money later had to buy back at interest. And then, in what I intended to be a quiet sideline and became something closer to an obsession, at the trading screen, where I found, to my genuine astonishment, a profession that violates every principle of preparation the other two rooms had beaten into me: no grading, no sequence, no development ladder, the deep end sold as the entry point, and the casualties blamed, with a straight face, for their mindset.

This book is what happened when I stopped being astonished and started writing down what all of those rooms had in common. It is not a book of setups; there are libraries of those, and their owners keep buying more of them, which tells you what they are worth without the right foundation beneath them. It is not a psychology book, though its final chapter has strong opinions about those. It is a book about order: the observation, tested across everything I have ever done competently, that consistency is a property of the sequence in which ordinary information is examined, and of nothing else, not talent, not information, not intensity, and certainly not prediction. Markets present the same picture to every participant. They always have. The difference was never in the picture.

I have called the chapters truths rather than laws, and the choice is deliberate. A law commands, and can be repealed, and invites the fantasy that the market is an authority with a rulebook to be memorized or a code to be cracked. A truth merely describes, cannot be repealed, and does not care whether you believe it: it simply sits there, collecting, with perfect patience, the accounts of those who trade against it. The twelve in this book were not invented; they were paid for, at market rates, and the tuition receipts are mine.

One more thing, and then the book can speak for itself. I publish under a name that is not mine, for professional reasons that are none of the book's business, and I am at ease with what that costs me: the trading shelf is crowded with biographies asking to be believed, and I have chosen to bring the one kind of book that does not need one. Nothing in these pages asks you to trust a résumé, and you should decline if it did, because a résumé is the should of publishing: a claim about what its owner's words ought to be worth. This book deals, like its second truth, only in what can be tested. It asks you to take a sequence, apply it to the same screen you looked at yesterday, and watch what the same information does when it is met in the right order. The sequence does not care who wrote it down. That is precisely why you can trust it.

Rowan Quill

HOW TO READ THIS BOOK

EACH CHAPTER ARGUES ONE truth, and every chapter is built the same way, on an old architecture borrowed from the tradition of laws-books. A Transgression: someone, usually great, destroyed by violating the truth. An Observance: someone who embodied it and collected. Keys: the truth put to work at the screen. An Image to remember it by, an Authority who said it before I did, and a Reversal, which may be the most important section of each chapter, because it records where the truth inverts, corrupts, or must be abandoned, and a doctrine without its reversal is just a dogma with better typography. The stories are there because principles without stories do not survive contact with a losing week; you will forget every abstraction in this book and remember the drop box, the plumb line, and the night watchman when it matters.

A word on the book's evidence, so that we have an honest contract. Where these pages say what most traders do, they speak from reasoned inference in the maxim tradition: years at the screen, years coaching performance, and the observed wreckage patterns of this industry, not from controlled studies. Where hard public numbers exist, the notes at the back point to them, and they are not kind to the deep end. The historical accounts are told from the standard published sources and were checked against them; where a story shades into legend, the text says so in place, with a tradition holds or a the story goes, and the two or three quotations that history attributes rather than records are labeled attributed exactly where they appear. A book about objective markers should submit to its own standard.

Be equally clear about the book's scope, because it is deliberate. These truths are instrument-agnostic and method-agnostic: they hold on any liquid market and any timeframe, and nothing in them will expire with this year's volatility. The cost of that durability is that the book tells you what must be done and in what order, and demonstrates it in five stylized worked readings, but does not hand you the particulars of your instrument: its tempos, its sessions' habits, the calibrations that turn a constitution into a working machine. Those are craft. Craft is learnable too, and it belongs to practice, and to the more particular teaching that lives beyond these pages. A book that pretended otherwise would be selling you the map's legend as the territory.

Read the chapters in order; each assumes its predecessors, the bridges between them are load-bearing, and the sequence of the book is itself the argument of the book. The appendix states the whole order on one page: it will mean little if you turn to it first, and everything once you have earned it. And the preface you may have skipped makes one promise worth repeating here: nothing in what follows requires you to predict anything, ever. If at any point you catch this book telling you what the market will do next, reread the sentence. It will be telling you what the market has done, and where, and when, and what that licenses you to do about it. The difference between those two sentences is the entire profession.

THE TWELVE TRUTHS

I. ORDER

The market presents the same picture to every participant. What separates the consistent from the erratic is not what they see but the order in which they see it. Examine information in the correct sequence and recurring setups reveal their mechanics. Examine it out of sequence and even accurate observations will conspire to mislead you. Master the order of seeing before you attempt to master anything else.

II. OBJECTIVITY

The market shows every participant the same picture, and it deceives no one. Distortion enters only at the eye. Anchor your judgment to what cannot be argued with: price, time, the range, the structure. Grant your opinion no authority it has not earned. The market knows only has and has not; the word should belongs to you, never to it. Strip should from your reading, and what remains is the market speaking plainly.

III. LOCATION

Price does not reward attention equally everywhere. It answers questions only at particular places; between them, it is merely traveling. Learn where the journey began, where price now stands, and where it is bound, in exact price, and the market's conduct becomes legible. Chase price through open country and you are guessing at speed. The trader is paid at locations. Everywhere else, he is the one paying.

IV. VALUE

Value is the reference from which every movement is measured. The market is not a battlefield where buyers and sellers wage war; it is an auction forever searching for the prices where business belongs. Learn to read where value lies within the current range, and where that range sits within the range that governs it, and every entry becomes one of two honest acts: buying at a discount, or selling at a premium. Everything else is paying retail.

V. TIME

Nothing in the market means anything except at its time. Price tells you what is being offered; only time tells you whether the offer is serious. The clock on your platform is not decoration, and it is not a code. It is the second of the market's two objective coordinates, ruled across every chart you will ever open. Read the market's calendar as plainly as its prices, and the day organizes itself: when to expect movement, when to expect nothing, and when the train departs for value.

VI. LANGUAGE

The market speaks all day to anyone equipped to listen. It does not prophesy; it reports. Structure, location, value, and time are its grammar. The candle is merely its alphabet. The task is never to predict what the market will say next; the task is to read, accurately and at the appointed moment, what it is saying now. Learn the difference. The first is gambling with extra steps. The second is the profession.

VII. FRAMING

No trade exists until it is framed. Before the market can answer you, three prices must stand in writing: where you act, where the idea dies, and where its work is done, together with the conditions under which the claim is valid at all. This is not caution. It is jurisprudence. An unframed trade is a case that never states its claim: it cannot be won, because nothing was ever at issue. Frame first. Then, and only then, are you permitted to be right.

VIII. MEASUREMENT

What cannot be measured cannot be managed, and what is merely desired can never be measured. The three prices of your frame are not chosen; they are surveyed, projected from structures the market itself has built. The account has needs, and the market has never once been informed of them. Derive every number from the ground, or watch the ground correct your arithmetic at your expense. In this business, the men who measure bury the men who wish.

IX. INVALIDATION

A stop belongs where price should not trade if your premise is intact: behind the accumulation that authored the move, beneath the swept liquidity that fueled it, outside the noise the journey ordinarily breathes. It is not a prediction of failure. It is the boundary at which the market has formally disagreed, and its placement is the most consequential measurement in trading. Dig the grave before the trade is born, and never once move it. Undug graves do not prevent death. They prevent burial, and the unburied kill the living.

X. REPETITION

The market never repeats its moves exactly, but never stops reflecting them. The next pullback borrows the character of the last; the coming leg is measured in the image of the one before; the journey underway inherits the habits of the campaign that authored it. Do not memorize the market's shape. Learn its gait. Shapes change with every session. The gait holds while the campaign holds, and when the gait breaks, the market has changed its mind about something, and so must you.

XI. PROCESS

You are not paid to be right. You are paid to operate a machine that harvests the market's journeys: a machine that files claims, buries the dead ones, collects at every station, and runs identically on its best day and its worst. Right and wrong are the vocabulary of spectators. Protect the account, pay the account along the way, and let the market keep the score it was always going to keep. The trade is an event. The process is the business.

XII. PSYCHOLOGY

The industry preaches that trading is mostly psychology, and then sells psychology as though it could be installed. It cannot. Confidence, patience, and discipline are not inputs a trader brings to the work; they are outputs the work produces when it is correctly ordered. Bad order makes bad psychology. Losses that cannot be explained manufacture fear; wins that cannot be repeated manufacture gamblers. Build the foundation in its sequence, and the mind the gurus keep promising will build itself.

A NOTE ON RISK

THIS BOOK DESCRIBES PROCESS, principle, and history. It is not investment, financial, or legal advice, and nothing in it is a recommendation to buy or sell any instrument. Trading involves substantial risk of loss and is not suitable for everyone; most people who attempt it lose money, a fact the notes at the back of this book document from public regulatory disclosures. The historical episodes recounted here are told for what they teach about process, not as guides to any market's future behavior. No representation is made that any reader will achieve results of any kind. Before trading, consider your circumstances and obtain advice from professionals who know them.

PART I

PERCEPTION

CHAPTER 1

ORDER

The Prospector's Sieve

The market presents the same picture to every participant. What separates the consistent from the erratic is not what they see but the order in which they see it. Examine information in the correct sequence and recurring setups reveal their mechanics. Examine it out of sequence and even accurate observations will conspire to mislead you. Master the order of seeing before you attempt to master anything else.

TRANSGRESSION OF THE TRUTH

IN THE SPRING OF 1796, a twenty-six-year-old general took command of a ragged, unpaid French army on the Italian frontier and within twelve months had shattered every force sent against him. Napoleon Bonaparte possessed what his contemporaries called coup d'œil, the stroke of the eye: the capacity to glance at a battlefield and grasp, in an instant, what mattered, in what order it mattered, and what must be done. At Austerlitz in December 1805 he deliberately weakened his own right flank to draw the Allied army down from the high ground of the Pratzen Heights, having already sequenced in his mind the entire chain of consequences that would follow. The Allies obliged, the French center took the heights behind them, and two empires were broken in a single afternoon. For a decade, this one mind out-processed entire councils of war.

But observe the structure of his supremacy, because it contained the seed of his destruction. Napoleon did not build a method. He was the method. What to examine first, what to weigh second, what to disregard entirely: this order lived in one skull and was written down nowhere. His chief of staff, Marshal Berthier, was a transmitting instrument of genius; he could convert the Emperor's intentions into precise written orders faster than any staff officer in Europe. But Berthier was never trained, and never permitted, to think in the Emperor's sequence. Neither was anyone else. Napoleon's marshals were fighting men, promoted for courage and dash and kept deliberately dependent. Whatever they could not ask him, they guessed.

As the empire grew, the volume of information grew past what one mind could order. In Russia in 1812 he commanded more than half a million men across a front of hundreds of miles. Reports arrived days old and out of order, contradicting one another. Decisions that had once been made from a hilltop with everything visible now had to be assembled from fragments, and the assembling system was one tired man. In 1813, fighting on several fronts at once, he continued to win the battles he personally directed, at Lützen, Bautzen, and Dresden, while the campaign as a whole disintegrated, because the marshals commanding elsewhere had no consistent way of examining their own situations. Each responded to whatever report arrived loudest and last.

The final act condensed the whole lesson into four days. In June 1815, Berthier was dead, having fallen from a window weeks before the campaign opened, and his replacement, Marshal Soult, was a fighting commander with little aptitude for staff work. On June 16, the corps of General d'Erlon, twenty thousand men, spent the entire day marching back and forth between two battlefields, Quatre Bras and Ligny, under contradictory orders, and fired scarcely a shot at either. Two days later, at Waterloo, Marshal Grouchy stood with some thirty-three thousand men a few miles from the decisive field, listening to the cannon. His written orders said one thing; the guns said another. His subordinate Gérard begged him to march to the sound of the firing. Grouchy had instructions, but he had no sequence for weighing them, no trained order that told him what to examine first when the picture changed. He followed the letter of the paper. Napoleon fought his last battle with a third of his army absent, and lost everything.

He did not lack information at Waterloo. He did not lack talent, even then. He lacked the one thing he had never troubled to build: an order for examining information that could exist outside his own head, an order that could function when he was tired, or absent, or wrong.

INTERPRETATION

NAPOLEON'S FATE EXPOSES THE most seductive error available to the gifted: mistaking a gift for a process. When the theater was small and his mind was fresh, the sequencing of information happened invisibly, at the speed of intuition, and it looked like magic. Because it looked like magic, he never examined it, never articulated it, and never transferred it. The moment scale, fatigue, and complexity exceeded the capacity of intuition, there was nothing underneath.

The market builds the same trap and baits it with early success. A trader begins with a feel for one instrument in one kind of condition, and wins. The winning convinces him that the feel is the edge. Then the conditions change, the size grows, the fatigue accumulates, and the feel, never having been written down as a sequence, cannot be repaired, because it was never understood. What cannot be stated as an order of examination cannot be repeated on demand. And what cannot be repeated on demand will abandon you at the precise moment the stakes are highest. That is not misfortune. It is architecture.

OBSERVANCE OF THE TRUTH

ON OCTOBER 14, 1806, the army of Frederick the Great, for half a century the most feared instrument in Europe, was annihilated by Napoleon in a single day, in the twin battles of Jena and Auerstedt. Fortresses that could have held for months surrendered in days; the kingdom of Prussia effectively collapsed in five weeks. Out of this humiliation, two officers, Gerhard von Scharnhorst and August von Gneisenau, drew the conclusion that nobody wanted to hear: Prussia had not been beaten by braver soldiers or better information. It had been beaten by one man's superior ordering of the same information everyone possessed. And since genius could not be requisitioned, they resolved to build something that made genius unnecessary.

Their instrument was the Prussian General Staff and the war academy that fed it. Officers selected for it were drilled in a fixed order of appreciation, applied to every situation without exception: first the terrain and the lines of communication; then the enemy's disposition and strength; only then their own means and the courses of action open to them. The conclusions officers reached could differ. The order in which they examined the situation could not. Staff officers were rotated between the staff and the line so that the sequence spread through the army's bloodstream, generation after generation, until it was no longer a doctrine but a reflex.

Helmuth von Moltke, who took charge of the General Staff in 1857, completed the design and then demonstrated it. In 1866, Prussia dispatched the Austrian Empire in seven weeks. In 1870 came the true test, against France, and here lies the detail that should trouble every trader who believes results come from better tools. The French infantry carried the Chassepot rifle, which outranged the Prussian needle gun by roughly double. The French possessed the mitrailleuse, an early machine gun the Prussians could not match. At the point of contact the French were better armed, and their soldiers fought with courage. France was broken in six weeks, and the French Emperor himself was taken prisoner at Sedan.

The difference was not information, and it was not armament. French commanders, brave, experienced, and individually capable, reacted to whichever report arrived loudest, improvising their priorities in the moment. Prussian commanders, most of them thoroughly average men, examined the same chaos in the same trained order and arrived at workable decisions faster, over and over, at every level of command. Because Moltke knew that every officer would sequence a situation identically, he could issue short directives stating his intent and trust distant subordinates to fill in the detail. Order did not suppress initiative. Order was precisely what made initiative safe to grant.

Within a generation, every major army on earth had copied the Prussian General Staff. It is worth pausing on the asymmetry: nobody copied Napoleon. Nobody could. A gift cannot be copied. A sequence can.

INTERPRETATION

THE PRUSSIANS UNDERSTOOD WHAT most traders spend their careers resisting: consistency is a property of sequence, not of talent, and sequence, unlike talent, can be built by anyone willing to submit to it. They did not attempt to out-genius the genius. They changed the terms of the contest: from inspiration, where they could not compete, to order, where the genius had never bothered to compete at all.

The French officer of 1870 is the retail trader of today: adequately informed, lavishly equipped, and reacting to whichever input shouts loudest. The sudden candle, the alert, the headline, the surge of momentum. The Prussian officer is the trader who has decided, in advance and in cold blood, the exact order in which the market will be examined, and who submits to that order on every occasion, under every condition. Note carefully what this trader has renounced: nothing, except improvisation in the one domain where improvisation ruins. You cannot manufacture genius. You can manufacture order. Only one of them is required.

KEYS TO THE TRUTH

EVERY TRADER KNOWS THE torment. The market keeps presenting the same setups: the breakout, the failed break, the reversal at a well-marked level. You have watched an identical setup succeed on Tuesday and fail on Thursday. And you have asked the only question that seems to matter. Why did it work then, and not now? So you interrogate the setup itself.

You measure it more finely. You find nothing. The answer was never inside the setup. Setups do not carry their own meaning. They inherit meaning from the conditions around them. And conditions can only be weighed in sequence. Run the same pattern through a different order of examination and you get a different trade, whatever it looks like on the chart. The pattern did not betray you. You were betrayed by the order in which you examined the world around it. That order changed between Tuesday and Thursday without your noticing. You never fixed it in the first place.

The market is the most democratic information system ever devised. Every participant sees the same price at the same moment. The same highs and lows. The same sessions, the same news. There is no privileged chart. Yet from identical information, a small minority extracts consistency while the majority extracts confusion. If information were the differentiator, that could not happen. The cure for inconsistency would simply be more information. The best-informed would be the most profitable. Every trader who bought a faster feed, added another indicator, and stayed inconsistent has personally disproven that theory. The difference is not the information. It is the order in which each mind processes it.

Understand what you are up against. The market does not present information in order of importance. It presents information in order of urgency. And urgency is a property of noise, not of significance. A sudden move demands attention. An alert demands attention. And whatever seizes your attention first does something worse than distract you. It becomes the frame through which you interpret everything you examine afterward. Psychologists call this anchoring. The first fact does not wait politely in a queue of evidence. It takes the judge's chair. Every later fact is heard as testimony for or against it.

Courts understood this centuries before psychologists named it. A trial is nothing more than a strict order of examination imposed on contested information. Rules dictate what a jury may hear, and in what sequence. They dictate what it may not hear at all until foundations are laid. Why? Because whoever frames the evidence first wins arguments he deserves to lose. The law does not trust twelve honest citizens to weigh testimony in whatever order it arrives. And their only task is judging a single case. You sit as judge and jury over hundreds of cases a year. Your own money is the defendant. And you grant yourself none of the same protection. Extend to your own perception the discipline the law extends to strangers.

This is why examining the market out of sequence corrupts even accurate observations. See the entry pattern first, and the higher-timeframe context you check afterward is no longer being read. It is being cross-examined for permission. The level is accurate. The momentum reading is accurate. The structure is drawn correctly. And every one of them has been recruited as a defense witness for a verdict you already delivered. Out of order, correct information does not merely lose its value. It changes sides.

The deepest studies of expertise all converge on this point. In the 1940s, a Dutch psychologist named Adriaan de Groot set out to find what separated grandmasters from strong club players. He was a chess master himself. The romantic assumption was calculation: the grandmaster simply sees more moves, further ahead. De Groot found nothing of the kind. The grandmasters examined barely more variations than the amateurs, and hardly deeper. What set them apart was the order of their perception. Show a grandmaster an unfamiliar position for a few seconds. He can rebuild it almost perfectly. The club player cannot. The master is not memorizing pieces. He is reading ordered structure: pawn chains, threats, coordination. He reads the board the way you read words rather than letters. Later researchers reran the experiment with pieces scattered randomly across the board, in positions that ordered perception could not parse. The grandmasters' advantage collapsed to almost nothing. Their superiority was never in how much they saw or calculated. It was in the sequence by which they saw. Structure before detail. Threat before opportunity. Position before calculation. Reverse that order and even a master will calculate variations that go nowhere while the mating threat sits in plain sight.

The same defense has been built wherever error is expensive, and always in the same shape. Aviation paid for it in blood: in 1935 the army's finest test pilot flew the most advanced aircraft yet built, the four-engined machine that would become the B-17, straight into the ground because he missed a single step, a control lock left unreleased. The response was not a more gifted pilot but a short printed list, a fixed order of attention imposed at exactly the moments when memory fails, and with that piece of paper the aircraft the newspapers had called unflyable became the backbone of a fleet. Medicine drills the identical reflex, history then examination then differential then tests, and forbids the diagnosis to close until the ordered evidence is in. And the United States, holding in the first days of December 1941 nearly every signal it needed, burned in an information-rich harbor because it had no system for weighing the fragments in order of significance. The domains do not resemble one another. The failure does, and so does the cure. It is never the information. It is the order in which the information is made to speak.

Now watch the same mechanics at a trading screen. Two traders open the same chart at the same moment. The first sees exactly what he has been hungry to see: a pattern he recognizes, at a level that has paid him before. Recognition produces conviction, and conviction goes shopping. He checks the higher timeframe and finds a way to read it as agreeable. He consults momentum; it can be squinted into alignment. He notes the session and the hour, and dismisses their objections. Every single observation is defensible. The conclusion is worthless. The examination ran backward, from verdict to evidence. Every fact was heard as testimony for a decision already made.

The second trader has given up the right to look at triggers first. She starts with the environment. Trending or ranging, and on which horizon? Then the map. Where has price come from? Where does it stand now? Is that location meaningful, or mere transit? Then the conditions. Do the session, the behavior, and the alignment justify interest at all? Only if each stage permits the next does she reach the question of an entry. Most days, the sequence stops her long before that. That is not a defect. It is the sequence doing its first job. An order of examination is, above all, a filter. And a filter that never rejects anything is not filtering.

Mark the deeper consequence, because it compounds for years. When the second trader loses, she can locate the step where the judgment failed. Environment misread. Location overrated. Condition absent. The loss becomes tuition: a correction applied to one step of a repeatable process. When the first trader loses, the loss teaches nothing. There is no fixed process to correct. So the loss gets filed as betrayal, bad luck, manipulation, noise. Both traders saw the same information. Order made one of them a perceiver and the other a rationalizer. Order made one history a data series and the other a pile of anecdotes. A trade examined in the same sequence as the hundred trades before it is a data point. You can draw conclusions from it. A trade examined in an improvised order belongs to no series at all. And no pile of such trades will ever add up to knowledge.

This is also why reading the market is a skill that some traders build and others merely wait for. Strip the mystique from technical analysis and it is rapid processing of a great deal of information under time pressure. It is finding the signal inside the noise in the minutes, sometimes the seconds, the market allows. That ability is trainable. But training has conditions. A skill is built from repetitions that resemble one another. And repetitions only resemble one another when they follow the same sequence. The pianist drills the same scale with the same fingering. He does not invent a new order of fingers each morning and call it practice. Ten thousand disordered repetitions do not produce mastery. They produce ten thousand separate experiences that never reinforce each other. A skill built on the wrong sequence, or on no sequence, cannot be mastered at all. What you are actually rehearsing is the disorder. The trader who examines his instrument in a fixed order is compounding one skill, year after year. The trader who examines it differently each day has been starting over every day, sometimes for decades. He calls the accumulated frustration experience.

There is another reason sequence is non-negotiable, and it is why the Prussians drilled theirs into reflex: pressure. Anyone can examine information patiently when nothing is at stake. Under fire, deliberation is the first casualty. In a fast market. In a drawdown. In the fever of a missed move. What remains is whatever you built into reflex. Pressure does not raise you to the occasion. It drops you onto whatever stands beneath you, and it finds nothing there that was not built in advance. Napoleon on his great days needed no system. Napoleon exhausted at Waterloo had nothing beneath the gift. And the gift was having an ordinary day. The Prussian officer under fire fell back into the drilled order, and the order caught him. Build the order in calm, for the hours when calm will not be available.

Expect to resist this truth. Everything in the trading temperament conspires against it. Traders come to markets for freedom, and sequence smells like bureaucracy. They trust inspiration, and sequence seems to insult it. Above all, the inconsistent trader prefers the flattering diagnosis: some critical piece of information is missing. A better indicator. A secret level. A faster feed. The honest diagnosis flatters no one. The information already in hand is being examined in the wrong order. The first diagnosis can be treated with a purchase. The second can only be treated with discipline. So he buys. And every new input added to a disordered process does not add clarity. It multiplies contamination: one more witness shouting for the anchor. The trader with twelve indicators consulted in no fixed order knows less than the trader with three consulted in strict order. Clarity was never a function of quantity. It is a function of sequence.

Order does not require you to ignore what arrives unannounced. New information will interrupt you: a headline, a sudden expansion, a level giving way ahead of schedule. The ordered trader has a place for every arrival. It enters the examination at the stage where it belongs. If the surprise strikes the environment, the sequence restarts from the top, calmly. Restarting is a known procedure. If it merely jostles the trigger, it waits its turn behind everything that outranks it. The disordered trader has no place to put anything. So everything lands on top of him. Each alert re-frames his entire view of the market. By the close he has held four opinions and executed none of them well. Order is not a wall against new information. It is a doorway with a doorman: everything may enter, but nothing chooses its own moment.

See what the sequence buys you on the mornings that matter most, when the open comes in fast and the screen is a riot. The disordered trader meets a fast open as a single overwhelming event, and does one of two things: freezes, or grabs. The ordered trader meets it as a queue. Environment: unchanged from last night's read, or visibly broken? Thirty seconds. Map: has the surge delivered price to a station, or flung it into transit? Ten more. Hour: this is the window itself; participation is present and the verdicts will be real ones. Value: where did the move leave us in the range? By the time the crowd's first impulse trades are being carried out on stretchers, the ordered trader has either found a claim worth framing or issued the else-nothing verdict, and both outcomes were reached through gates, not through nerve. Speed does not break a true sequence. Speed is where a true sequence finally shows what it was built for.

So put the question to yourself, and answer without rehearsal. When you open your instrument, what do you examine first? What second, third, fourth? Not your rules. Not your setups. The fundamental data that drives every market and stands in plain sight on every chart: price itself, the session and the hour, the prevailing behavior, the structure. If the answer does not come instantly, in a fixed order you could recite with your eyes closed, you have found the explanation for years of inconsistent results. It was never the setups. And understand what the right order buys you. It is far more than tidiness. Data points examined in their proper sequence stop being a crowd of facts. They become a chain of confirmation. Each one extends the developing picture or breaks it. Price starts making sense at the exact moment it confirms or denies what the previous step taught you to expect. The guesswork and emotion that attend most trades erode, because nothing is being guessed. No single data point outranks the others. The rank lives in the order of their consideration. That is the entire mechanism by which signal is separated from noise. And it costs nothing but obedience.

Be equally clear about what order is not. It is not a strategy, and it is not a promise. The market owes your sequence nothing on any given trade. Two disciplined traders can keep different sequences and both prosper, provided each keeps his own without exception. The content of a sound order will assemble itself through the truths that follow. Weigh the general environment before the particular level. Establish where price stands before asking what it might do. State the conditions of a trade's validity before its trigger. Know the point where the idea dies before the idea is acted on. For now, secure the foundation beneath all of them. Whatever you examine, examine it in the same order every time. Context before detail. Conditions before conclusions. Environment before entry. And treat any breach of your order as an error, whatever the outcome of the trade. Profit taken from a disordered decision is the most expensive money you will ever accept. It pays you to abandon the sequence, and the market will collect that debt with interest.

IMAGE

The Prospector's Sieve. The river carries gold and gravel together, and it offers both to every hand on its banks equally. One man plunges in wherever the water glitters, and lifts out mud. Another passes the same water through a series of meshes, always the coarsest first, always the finest last, and the gold cannot help but be found. The river does not decide who prospers. The order of the mesh decides.

AUTHORITY

"The third [rule was] to conduct my thoughts in such order that, by commencing with objects the simplest and easiest to know, I might ascend little by little, and, as it were, step by step, to the knowledge of the more complex." — René Descartes, Discourse on Method, 1637

REVERSAL

ORDER HAS ITS OWN transgression, and it must be guarded against as vigilantly as chaos. The first corruption is ritual: the sequence performed as ceremony, each step ticked without perception, the checklist mistaken for the seeing it was built to protect. The Prussian system itself decayed this way. In later generations, the heirs of Moltke hardened his living method into iron timetables and inflexible plans, and in 1914 order without perception marched a continent into catastrophe. Moltke himself had left the warning in plain sight: no plan of operations, he wrote, extends with any certainty beyond the first contact with the enemy's main strength. The father of systematic order refused to worship it. The sequence exists to direct your attention, never to replace it. The moment you complete your order of examination without having actually seen anything, you have kept the ritual and lost the religion.

The second misreading is to confuse order with slowness. A sequence practiced ten thousand times at deliberate speed compresses; it does not disappear. The master's checklist runs in seconds precisely because it once ran in minutes, thousands of times over. If your order collapses whenever the market speeds up, it was memorized, not internalized: a script, not a reflex. The remedy is more repetition, not less order. And when genuine novelty arrives, the shock that fits no category, the ordered mind is the only one that can even recognize it as novel. The disordered mind has never seen anything clearly enough to know when it is seeing something new.

Before this chapter closes, gather up how much work the one word has been doing, because the word was chosen for its reach, and the book will now spell it with a capital letter. Order is, first, an approach of mind: the trader who submits to it agrees to examine before wanting, to see before concluding, and to let conviction arrive last instead of first. Order is, second, a property of information: the same facts, taken in a different order, manufacture a different trader, as every anchored judge and every checklist pilot in this chapter has testified. Order is, third, a property of the market itself: price is not scattered, it travels and ranges and returns on structure that repeats at every magnification, and the chapters ahead exist to map it. And order is, last, an act of acceptance: before any procedure can save you, you must concede that a procedure is required, which is the concession the Emperor never made and the Prussians built an institution upon. Hold the four together and they resolve into a single distinction that governs the rest of this book. The Order is the state: the law the market keeps and the discipline the trader submits to. The Sequence is the steps: the Order performed at the screen, one gate at a time. The twelve truths build the first. The appendix states the second.

Nothing becomes reliable until it is placed in the right order. But order is a servant with a single master, and that master is accurate perception. An immaculate sequence applied to a distorted picture merely organizes the distortion. Before the order of seeing can serve you, the eye itself must be cleaned. That is the work of the second truth: Objectivity.

CHAPTER 2

OBJECTIVITY

The Climber's Ladder

The market shows every participant the same picture, and it deceives no one. Distortion enters only at the eye. Anchor your judgment to what cannot be argued with: price, time, the range, the structure. Grant your opinion no authority it has not earned. The market knows only has and has not; the word should belongs to you, never to it. Strip should from your reading, and what remains is the market speaking plainly.

TRANSGRESSION OF THE TRUTH

THERE HAS PERHAPS NEVER lived a mind more capable of objectivity than Isaac Newton's. He had weighed the light of the sun, calculated the orbits of comets, and reduced the motion of the planets to a handful of laws that held across the whole of the visible heavens. He was, by 1720, not only the most celebrated natural philosopher in the world but a wealthy and practical man of affairs, Master of the Royal Mint, a person who dealt daily in gold and coin and understood money as few scholars ever have. If objectivity were a faculty of intelligence, Newton would have been immune to what followed. He was not. He was ruined, and the manner of his ruin is the most instructive story in the history of speculation.

Newton held stock in the South Sea Company, whose shares through the first half of 1720 rose in one of the great manias of the age. In the spring, with the price already high and still climbing, Newton did the objective thing. He sold. He took his profit, reckoned by the most careful modern accounting at some twenty thousand pounds, a doubling of his money and a sober reading of an unsustainable rise. Had the story ended there, he would appear in these pages as an exemplar rather than a warning. It did not end there. Through the summer the price did not fall as reason demanded. It roughly trebled. And Newton, watching from the sidelines while men of a fraction of his intellect grew rich around him, watched the one thing no objective marker can survive begin to work on him: the sight of other people making money.

He re-entered. He bought back into the company near the height of the frenzy, and he bought heavily, committing far more than the profit he had prudently banked in the spring. Within months the South Sea Bubble burst, as every such structure must, and the price collapsed toward its foundations. Newton did not sell into the fall. He held, in the way that a man holds who cannot bear to convert a paper loss into a real one, and by the time the wreckage settled he had lost something like twenty thousand pounds, a fortune that would run well into the millions in today's money. He is said to have forbidden the very words South Sea to be spoken in his presence for the rest of his life.

The remark posterity fixed to him, that he could calculate the motions of the heavenly bodies but not the madness of men, is very probably something he never actually said. It has survived for three centuries anyway, because it describes something true about him that is worth more than its authenticity. The most objective intellect of his era was undone not by a failure of calculation but by a failure of objectivity: he abandoned his own correct reading of the evidence the moment his ego could no longer tolerate watching others prosper. The data had not changed. He had.

INTERPRETATION

NEWTON'S RUIN DISMANTLES THE most comfortable excuse in trading: that objectivity is a matter of intelligence, and that the losing trader simply needs to think harder or know more. Newton thought harder than anyone alive and knew more than almost anyone who has ever lived. It did not save him, because the thing that failed in him was not his intellect. It was his willingness to keep obeying evidence that had stopped flattering him. Objectivity is not a level of intelligence. It is a discipline of allegiance, a decision about what you will take your orders from, and it can be broken in an instant by a mind of any size.

Observe precisely where he broke. Not in the spring, when he read the evidence and acted on it, but in the summer, when the evidence still said the same thing and the sight of other men's gains said something louder. This is the exact mechanism that empties trading accounts. It is rarely the absence of a correct reading. It is the surrender of a correct reading to something that is not evidence at all: envy, boredom, the ache of watching a move go on without you. The market did not take Newton's fortune. His ego took it, and used the market as the instrument. What you will learn to guard is not your analysis. It is your allegiance to your analysis when everything in you wants to defect.

OBSERVANCE OF THE TRUTH

CHARLES DARWIN WAS NOT a genius in the Newtonian mold, and he knew it. He described himself as an ordinary man of ordinary abilities, and by raw intellectual candlepower he was almost certainly right. Yet he constructed one of the most durable theories in the history of science, a theory that has survived a century and a half of the most determined attack, and he did it not by being cleverer than his opponents but by building a machine for objectivity and submitting to it without exception for twenty years.

The machine was a habit, and Darwin described it plainly in his autobiography as a golden rule. Whenever he encountered a published fact, a fresh observation, or a stray thought that ran contrary to his emerging theory, he forced himself to write it down at once, immediately, without fail. He had discovered by hard experience the thing that ought to be carved above every trading desk: that facts and thoughts which contradict our conclusions are far more apt to slip from memory than the ones that confirm them. The agreeable evidence sticks without effort. The inconvenient evidence evaporates unless it is nailed down the moment it appears. So Darwin nailed it down. He kept his contradictions in writing, where his memory could not quietly dispose of them, and he made himself confront the strongest case against his own idea before he would trust the idea at all.

Consider the restraint this required. Darwin conceived the essential mechanism of natural selection in 1838. He did not publish On the Origin of Species until 1859. For more than twenty years he assembled objections and answered them, bred pigeons, dissected barnacles for eight years, corresponded with breeders and gardeners and anyone who might furnish a fact that could break his theory, and only when he had hunted down every contrary observation he could find and it had failed to destroy him did he commit. He did not fall in love with his conclusion and then defend it. He tried to murder it, methodically, for two decades, and published only what survived. And the discipline nearly cost him everything: in June of 1858 a letter reached him from a naturalist in the Malay islands, Alfred Russel Wallace, sketching in a few fevered pages the very theory Darwin had spent twenty years perfecting. Two decades of golden-rule caution had brought him within a courtesy of being scooped by a younger man's essay; the affair was settled honorably with a joint reading, and Darwin raced his book to press the next year. Mark the lesson in both directions, because this book will need both: test your idea against everything, and know that even the best-tested claim carries an expiry, for the world, like the market, pays the one who files.

The result is the signature of true objectivity, and it is worth stating precisely, because it is the opposite of what the anxious trader believes objectivity feels like. Darwin was not paralyzed by his even-handedness. He committed with enormous force, staked his life's reputation on a single controversial idea, and turned out to be right. His long neutrality toward the evidence did not weaken his eventual conviction. It was the foundation of it. He could hold his theory without flinching precisely because he had already met, and recorded, and answered every marker that stood against it.

INTERPRETATION

DARWIN'S GOLDEN RULE IS not a moral virtue. It is a procedure, mechanical and transferable, and that is exactly why it belongs in a book about process rather than a book about character. He did not trust himself to be objective. No one should. He knew that his own memory was a biased instrument that would preserve the flattering fact and lose the threatening one, and rather than resolve to try harder, which never works, he built an external system that did the remembering for him. The writing down was the whole of it. What is committed to the record cannot be quietly forgotten when it becomes inconvenient.

The trader's version writes itself. The evidence that agrees with your bias will present itself loudly and lodge in memory without effort; the evidence that threatens your bias will appear once, quietly, and be gone by the time you need it. If you rely on your recollection to stay balanced, you will remember a distorted market, weighted entirely toward the position you already hold. The remedy is not to be more honest. It is to externalize the honesty, to record the markers against your idea as faithfully as the markers for it, so that the disagreement survives long enough to be weighed. Objectivity that lives only in the mind does not exist. It has to live somewhere the ego cannot reach in to edit it.

KEYS TO THE TRUTH

BEGIN WITH THE FACT that makes objectivity possible at all. The market is the rare arena in which the primary evidence is genuinely, verifiably objective. Ask any two people on earth what price an instrument last traded at. They will give you the same number. Ask them the high of the day, the low, the open, the close. Ask them the boundaries of the session's range. They will agree, because these are not opinions. They are records. Price is the purest objective marker in any field of human decision. Everyone can see it, and no one can honestly dispute it. This is a gift most disciplines never receive. The physician must infer the disease behind the symptoms. The general must guess at the enemy behind the hill. The trader is handed, continuously and for free, a stream of facts that require no interpretation to exist. And then, astonishingly, he sets about burying that gift under a heap of his own invention.

The burial has a pattern. Once you see it, you cannot unsee it. Objective markers do not all sit at the same distance from the truth. They lie along a spectrum, and reliability falls at every step away from the raw record. Price itself is bedrock. The day's open, high, low, and close are bedrock. The boundaries of a completed range are near-bedrock. So is the edge of a gap, and so is a level that price has objectively touched or not touched. These are disputable only at the margins. Market structure stands with them, though it asks more of the observer. Structure is read, not merely seen. There is a right way, a wrong way, and a no way to read it. Two trained observers mark the same swings identically. When two traders disagree about structure, the disagreement is evidence about the training, never about the structure. The structure sits on the chart as objectively as the prices that built it. A later truth returns to this. The ground first softens further out, at indicators. Indicators feel objective because a machine computes them and renders them as a precise line. They are nothing of the kind. An indicator is an interpretation wearing the costume of a fact. It lags, because it is built from prices that have already occurred. It also carries a whole method of interpretation folded invisibly inside its formula, chosen by whoever designed it. At the far end of the spectrum, past all the markers, sits pure opinion. Overextended, exhausted, toppy, due. These are not readings of the market. They are readings of the trader.

Here is the test that sorts the objective from the subjective. Apply it to every element of your analysis without mercy. Would two informed observers, shown the same chart, record this identically? If the answer is yes, you are standing on objective ground. It is yes for price, for the range, for the gap, for the touched or untouched level. Suppose the answer is no, and the two observers could reasonably disagree. Then what you are looking at is interpretation. It must be demoted to the rank of interpretation no matter how strongly you feel it. The word overextended fails this test instantly. One trader's overextended is another's barely begun. There is no line on the chart that everyone agrees marks the place. Catch yourself reasoning from a word that would fail the two-observer test. In that moment you have caught yourself substituting your ego for the market.

That substitution has a single, sovereign tell. If you learn to hear only one word in your own trading mind, make it this one. The word is should. The market should turn here. Price should not be able to break this level. It should reverse. It is too far, too fast, too high. Should is the sound of the ego overruling the evidence. It has no referent in anything on the chart. It refers only to what the trader wants, or expects, or has bet on. The market does not deal in should. It deals in two conditions only, has and has not. Price has reached the level, or it has not. The range has broken, or it has not. The marker you required has appeared, or it has not. Every should in your reading marks a place where you have stopped observing the market and started negotiating with it. And the market does not negotiate. Strike the word from your working vocabulary. Replace should turn with has not yet shown a single marker of turning. Then watch what happens: the false certainty drains out. You are returned to the evidence, which is the only place you were ever safe.

None of this means you may not hold a view. You must hold a view. A trader without a bias is not objective, merely idle. This chapter will return to that point. But a bias has a proper station, and that station is subordinate. Your bias is a framing of what is possible. It is a hypothesis about what the market may be preparing to do. It is permitted to direct your attention. It is never permitted to override the markers. The mechanism that keeps it in its place is the one Newton abandoned and Darwin institutionalized. You require the market to confirm your bias, objectively, marker by marker, before you trust it. You hold yourself ready to abandon it the instant the markers refuse to appear. Picture a ladder. The bias is the direction you intend to climb. But you may put your weight only on rungs that actually exist beneath your hand. Each objective marker that appears as your idea plays out is a rung. You ascend from one to the next, confirmed at every step. Suppose you reach the top and the trade has worked. You were not right because you hoped, or because you assessed cleverly. You were not right because a candle turned green, or because the price was moving your way. You were right because the rungs appeared, one after another. They appeared exactly as your experience told you they must if the idea were sound. And on the days the rungs do not appear, you do not climb. You do not reach for a rung that is not there and trust your weight to it. That is not conviction. That is falling.

This is also the deep reason that good trading is boring. Boredom is not a defect of the objective method but its signature. The astronomers learned this two centuries ago. Their story is the cleanest proof that the fault lies in the eye and not in the world. In 1796 the Astronomer Royal, Nevil Maskelyne, dismissed his assistant David Kinnebrook from the Greenwich Observatory. The young man's offense was small. His recorded times for stars crossing the meridian ran later than Maskelyne's own. The gap was about half a second at first, then roughly eight tenths of a second. He seemed unable to correct the habit however he tried. Maskelyne assumed his own eye was the true one and the assistant's was faulty. He let him go, though he called him diligent and useful. The assumption was wrong, and the error was profound. Decades later the German astronomer Friedrich Bessel wondered whether any two observers would differ in the same way. He compared himself against other astronomers of the first rank. He found discrepancies larger than the one that had cost Kinnebrook his post. There was no faulty observer. Every observer was faulty, each in his own consistent direction. The eye itself, even a trained and honest eye, imposes a personal distortion on what it records.

Note carefully what astronomy did with this discovery. It is precisely what the objective trader must do. Astronomy did not exhort its observers to try harder to be unbiased. The whole point was that effort could not reach the error. The error operated below the level of will. Instead astronomy measured the distortion and corrected for it. Ultimately it replaced the fallible human reflex with instruments wherever it could. The remedy for subjective distortion was never more sincerity. It was more objective markers, and less reliance on the eye. So it is in trading. The more skilled you become, the more you should be leaning on the objective record. Lean less on your own impression of it. In the end your judgment should consist almost entirely of reading markers that anyone could verify. It should consist almost not at all of the intuitive flourishes that feel, to the ego, like skill. We resist this because we love to bring ourselves to the process. Our own flavor, our own cleverness, our own feel for the tape. That flavor is Kinnebrook's half-second. It feels like insight and it functions like error. The discipline of a lifetime is the steady removal of it.

The whole doctrine resolves into a single scene. Same chart, same morning, and, for once, the same bias in two different heads. Both believe the market is likely to turn at a zone overhead. Both are, so far, doing nothing wrong, because a bias honestly held is permitted. Price rises into the zone. The first trader feels the pull of the level. He feels the ache of the profit he will miss if he waits. He hears himself think the fatal word: it should turn here. He sells. He is not reading the market. He is asserting a wish about it. He has trusted his weight to a rung that does not yet exist. Price pushes through the zone as if it were not there. Now the second, more expensive stage begins. The man who entered on should cannot easily exit on should either. Every marker now says the idea has failed. But his ego, having committed, hears only that price is even more overextended than before. Even more due to turn. So he holds, and he adds, exactly as Newton held and added. He converts a small error of objectivity into a ruinous one.

The second trader holds the identical bias and does the opposite thing with it. The difference is entirely a difference of allegiance. She has decided in advance which objective markers the market must produce if her idea is sound. These are the specific signatures her experience tells her accompany a genuine turn at such a zone. She has resolved to do nothing until they appear. Price rises into the zone. She does not sell, because the zone is not a marker. It is merely the place her bias pointed her attention. She waits for the market to speak in the only grammar she trusts, has and has not. If the markers appear, one after another, she acts. Then she is right for the only reason worth being right. The evidence confirmed the idea rung by rung. If the markers do not appear, she does nothing at all. She takes no loss and feels no regret, because she was never owed the trade. Most days, this is how it ends: with no trade. She has not missed anything. She has declined to fall. The first trader will call her passive and call himself decisive. He will do so right up until the accounting, which is the only judge either of them will ever answer to.

The distance between these two traders is not knowledge. It is not intelligence. It is certainly not conviction, of which the first trader had a dangerous surplus. It is the single decision about what they take their orders from. The first takes his orders from should. He takes them from the inside of his own head, from the picture of the market he wishes were true. The second takes her orders from has. She takes them from the record, from the markers anyone could verify. This is the whole of objectivity. It is available to any trader of any ability on any day. It costs nothing but the surrender of the ego's right to overrule the evidence. That surrender is the hardest thing in trading. No quantity of study substitutes for it. The market is forever offering you the chance to be Newton in the spring, who read the evidence and obeyed it. Or Newton in the summer, who read the same evidence and obeyed his envy instead. The chart will not tell you which one you are being. Only the word in your mind will, and the word is either has or should.

IMAGE

The Climber's Ladder. The climber knows which peak he intends to reach, and the intention is good, for it points him upward. But he puts his weight only on rungs his hand can close around. Where a rung exists, he rises; where none does, he waits, or he descends. The mountain does not care where he wishes to stand. It holds only the men who trusted their weight to what was actually there. Hope has never once borne the weight of a climber.

AUTHORITY

"The first principle is that you must not fool yourself—and you are the easiest person to fool." — Richard Feynman, Caltech commencement address, 1974

REVERSAL

OBJECTIVITY HAS A FALSE twin, and it wears the same clothes, and it is more dangerous to the thoughtful trader than raw bias precisely because it looks like virtue. The false twin is the belief that objectivity means holding no opinion, committing to nothing, waiting for a certainty the market never supplies. This is not objectivity; it is paralysis with good posture. The market never presents a fact that is also a guarantee. Every trade is an act of commitment under irreducible uncertainty, and the trader who refuses to commit until the evidence is beyond all doubt will commit to nothing, ever, because that moment does not arrive. Darwin was not neutral about his theory in the end. He staked everything on it. His objectivity was the discipline that earned him the right to that conviction, not a substitute for having any. Objectivity governs how you form and test a view. It does not excuse you from holding one.

There is a subtler corruption, and it is the one to fear most, because the objective trader is its natural prey. It is the dressing of a subjective wish in objective clothing: drawing the level where your bias needs it rather than where price actually put it, selecting the timeframe on which the market agrees with you and calling that the real one, counting the markers that confirm and overlooking with perfect sincerity the ones that do not. This is Kinnebrook's error committed on purpose and then hidden from oneself, and no amount of raw honesty prevents it, because it feels exactly like objectivity from the inside. Only Darwin's remedy defeats it: the external record, the marker written down before the outcome is known, the contrary evidence nailed to the page where the ego cannot quietly revise it. Objectivity is not a state of mind you can achieve and then possess. It is a structure you build outside your mind, because the mind is the very thing that cannot be trusted to police itself.

The eye can be cleaned, then, but never made perfect, and the honest trader works forever at the cleaning while acting decisively on what the imperfect eye can still verify. A clean eye, though, only tells you what is true. It does not yet tell you where to look, and the market is mostly empty space in which even perfect vision finds nothing worth trading. Sight must now be pointed at the places that matter. That is the third truth: Location.

THE TRUTHS AT WORK

A FIRST READING

THE SAME MORNING, TWICE

This first reading is the Sequence's opening law, watched before any gate has been given its name: that the order in which a market is examined decides everything the examination will find.

BEFORE THE TRUTHS OF terrain arrive, watch the two you already hold do a morning's work on their own. The scene is deliberately ordinary and deliberately stylized. No instrument is named. Every price is in plain points, because the lesson is the reading, not the market. An instrument has drifted higher overnight and opens the session a little above yesterday's close. On the small timeframes, a tidy flag is forming near the highs, the pattern every primer teaches. Momentum is bright, and the feed is enthusiastic. Two traders sit down to the identical picture.

The first begins where his eye lands, on the flag. He knows this picture. A strong leg climbed through yesterday, the expansion every primer calls the pole, and now price rests in a tidy consolidation beneath the highs. He reads the little range the way he was taught to read it. Its highs are the bears' line. Its lows are the bulls' line. Every candle inside it is a skirmish in a battle of orders, and he keeps score. Each dip that gets bought confirms him. Each push that stalls he forgives. He came to this chart already long in his mind, because the prior move was up and his bias rode in with it, and the flag now performs its true function, which is not information. It is justification. He picks the bulls because he had already picked them, enters at the flag's edge with the stop tucked beneath it, and settles in to be paid for his pattern knowledge. His examination ran backward, from conviction to evidence. You have met him in every chapter. Whatever happens next will teach him nothing.

Hold that picture, because it is the exact photographic negative of the second truth. Objectivity is not the absence of a view. The second trader also carries a bias this morning, and his bias is also long. The difference is the direction of the current. The first trader tells the market what the flag means. The second trader lets price and its objective markers tell him whether the journey he supposes is actually occurring. One instructs the tape. The other consents to be instructed by it.

The second trader runs the sequence, and the demonstration is how far it travels without one word of prophecy. He begins at the origin. Where did this journey start, what authored it, and what route does it imply. The chapters ahead will give the places on that route their proper names, the stations and the sub-locations between them, so watch the method now and learn the map later. Along the route he asks one question at each expected place. Did price arrive where the journey said it should, and when it arrived, did the structure speak. At a true sub-location the market announces itself in printed verdicts, and the announcement points one of two ways. Onward, toward the next sub-location, where a toll might be collected. Or no further, toward the counter prime location, the destination that stands just before a reversal.

Then the appraisal. Within its own small range, this morning's price sits high. Within the governing range above it, the reading is the same. Premium inside premium, dear within dear, and the fourth truth will have much to say about buying there. He measures the sub-location where price now resists, and its components are objective and few. The prior swing high above was taken in the overnight drift and has not held above it since. That is a verdict, printed, and printed against the enthusiasm. At that exact price the signatures repeat, wicks through and closes back inside, the mark of a train that is unlikely to proceed. And the clock has a vote as well. The hour is approaching when participation arrives in volume, the window where this market keeps its habit of turning for short-term corrections. Five observations, every one of them a has or a has not, and not one of them supports the long he would prefer to take. The flag is real. The case is not. He stands down in a handful of minutes, and his attention is scheduled for the sub-location below, where a correction would finally make prices legible.

The morning obliges with a lesson. The flag breaks upward, exactly as the first trader's primer promised, and for a few minutes he is paid. Then the break fails. Price pushes above the swept high, cannot hold there either, and reverses sharply, running down through the flag, through the first trader's stop, and on to the sub-location below. Note carefully what the second trader does with this information. Nothing. He held every objective reason to sell the failure, and a different book would praise him for taking it. He does not, because his governing read is still up, and his discipline is not a machine for taking every trade the tape offers. It is a machine for taking his. Objectivity bought him two things this morning. It kept him out of a false breakout that punished conviction. And it delivered him, at better value and at a legible place, to the platform where he will board the train toward the prime location above.

Notice everything this reading did not require. No forecast, and no argument with the first trader, who on another morning may well be paid, because on any single morning the market can reward disorder, and that is its favorite trap. The first truth already named that reward the most expensive money you will ever accept. Run both mornings a hundred times and the two traders no longer share a profession. One has a pile of anecdotes about flags and a stop-out he still blames on manipulation. The other has a data series, a filter that worked, and a scheduled appointment the market kept. The same information, twice, and the order of examination was the entire difference. That is the only point this first reading exists to prove.

Name, now, the gates this reading walked without naming them. It began at the map, asking where price had come from and where the route implied it was going. It weighed the value and found premium inside premium. It consulted the clock. It waited for the market to sign, and read the printed verdicts when it did. It framed nothing, because the reading never earned a frame, and that refusal is the Sequence too. The chapters ahead give each of these gates its proper name and its fixed place. Here you have only watched them open in order, which was the single thing that made one trader's morning legible and left the other's a heap of anecdotes.

PART II

ORIENTATION

CHAPTER 3

LOCATION

The Waterhole

Price does not reward attention equally everywhere. It answers questions only at particular places; between them, it is merely traveling. Learn where the journey began, where price now stands, and where it is bound, in exact price, and the market's conduct becomes legible. Chase price through open country and you are guessing at speed. The trader is paid at locations. Everywhere else, he is the one paying.

TRANSGRESSION OF THE TRUTH

ON THE THIRD DAY of July, 1863, on a low ridge in Pennsylvania, the most admired commander of his age destroyed the finest infantry he would ever lead, and he did it in about an hour. For two years Robert E. Lee had beaten larger, better-supplied armies through sheer audacity. Two months earlier, at Chancellorsville, outnumbered two to one, he had divided his army in the face of the enemy, flung half of it through supposedly impassable woods, and routed a force twice his size. Boldness had never failed him. Now he stood deep in enemy territory at Gettysburg, after two days of fighting in which his attacks on the Union flanks had broken against hills and rocky ground, and he resolved to settle the matter with one great blow at the center.

The plan required roughly twelve and a half thousand men, under Pickett, Pettigrew, and Trimble, to march across nearly a mile of open, gently rising farmland toward Cemetery Ridge, where the Union army waited behind a stone wall on higher ground, its artillery converging on every acre of the approach. James Longstreet, Lee's senior corps commander, protested; he later wrote that he told Lee no fifteen thousand men ever arrayed for battle could take that position. Lee was unmoved. The enemy was there, and he would strike him there. The preliminary bombardment, the greatest of the war, sailed largely over the Union line and spent itself in the fields beyond. Then the guns fell quiet, and the gray lines stepped out of the trees in parade order and began to walk.

What followed was not a battle but an equation working itself out. Union artillery tore the formations from the front and both flanks while rifled muskets waited behind the wall. The brigades crossed the fields and melted as they crossed. A few hundred men under Lewis Armistead reached the wall at a copse of trees and held a patch of ground for a few minutes before they were killed or taken. More than half the attacking force was lost inside the hour. Lee rode out among the survivors repeating that it was all his fault, and he was right. The place where Armistead fell is still called the high-water mark of the Confederacy. The army that made the charge never mounted a great offensive again.

Mark what had changed between Chancellorsville and Gettysburg, because it was not Lee. The men were the same men, the general the same general, the conviction the same conviction. The audacity that had been genius on one field was annihilation on another, and the entire difference was location. At Chancellorsville the ground had multiplied his boldness; at Gettysburg the ground converted boldness into casualties at a fixed rate of exchange, and no quality of soldier or commander could alter the rate. Lee had asked the question of his enemy, when the mile of open field had already answered it.

INTERPRETATION

CONVICTION DOES NOT NEGOTIATE with ground. Lee's failure has a precise structure: he decided what he wished to do, and then required the location to accommodate the wish. The location declined. Traders repeat this structure daily. An idea forms, conviction hardens, and the trade is executed wherever price happens to be when the conviction peaks, as though the quality of the idea could compensate for the poverty of the place. It cannot. The market, like the battlefield, charges a different price for the same action in different places. An entry is never merely an idea. It is an idea at a location, and of the two, the location is senior.

Note also what past success had taught Lee, because it teaches traders the same corrupt lesson. Audacity had always paid him, so audacity became the plan itself. But what had actually paid at Chancellorsville was audacity on favorable ground; the ground was the silent partner in every victory, and when the partner withdrew, the profits went with it. The trader who has won by aggression in one set of conditions concludes that aggression is his edge, and he carries it everywhere, onto any field, at any price. He credits himself in the good places and curses his luck in the bad ones, and never isolates the variable that was deciding all along: not the manner of the attack, but the ground on which it was made.

OBSERVANCE OF THE TRUTH

ARTHUR WELLESLEY, DUKE OF Wellington, commanded armies for two decades against the greatest military power of the age and never lost a major battle. He had little of Napoleon's dash and none of his theatrical genius, and he knew it. His mastery lay elsewhere, in something so unglamorous that his enemies mistook it for timidity until it was too late: he was the supreme reader of ground in the history of his profession. He rode the country himself, studied it through his glass for hours, remembered ridgelines the way bankers remember balances, and marked positions years before he needed them. His signature device, the reverse slope, was simplicity itself: he placed his infantry behind the crest of a ridge, out of sight and out of the line of fire, while the enemy climbed toward an empty skyline that told them nothing. The attacking columns deployed blind and breathless; his men stood up at fifty paces, delivered their volleys, and the ground itself had done half the killing.

In 1810, facing Masséna's invasion of Portugal with a smaller army, Wellington gave the fullest demonstration of the truth. He did not offer battle at the frontier. He withdrew, stripping the country bare as he went, into the Lines of Torres Vedras: three belts of fortifications built in near secrecy across the peninsula north of Lisbon, more than a hundred redoubts sewn from ridge to ridge to the sea. Masséna arrived, studied the ground, and refused to attack it. There was nothing else to attack. For months one of the finest armies in Europe sat in front of the lines and starved, and when it finally staggered back toward Spain it had lost some twenty-five thousand men, almost without a battle worth the name. Wellington had won one of the decisive strategic victories of the age while declining, nearly absolutely, to fight.

Understand what made this observance rather than mere caution. Wellington was offered battle constantly, on ground that did not suit him, and he refused it constantly: retreating, waiting, marching away, indifferent to the murmuring of younger officers who wanted glory and called him overcareful. He grasped what they did not: that refusing battle on bad ground is not the absence of strategy but its very essence, because every engagement declined at a disadvantage preserved the army for the place where the advantage would be his. His force was finite, Britain's only field army, and he spent it the way a miser spends capital: nowhere, until the ground promised a return, and then all at once.

At the end, facing Napoleon himself, he did what he had done his whole career. He placed his army on a ridge at Mont-Saint-Jean, a position he had noted and filed away long before, put his infantry behind the crest in the old manner, and stood still. The greatest attacking army in Europe broke itself climbing toward that quiet skyline. The commander who never lost had spent twenty years proving a single proposition:

choose where, and the ground will help you win; let the enemy choose where, and you must beat the enemy and the ground together.

INTERPRETATION

WELLINGTON'S DISCIPLINE TRANSLATES TO the trading screen without remainder. He did not fight because the enemy was near, or because the day was convenient, or because his blood was up, or because he had not fought in a while. He fought where the ground multiplied his force, and elsewhere he did the thing most traders find impossible: nothing. The waiting was not passivity. It was the active preservation of finite capital for the locations where capital counts, and it looked like weakness right up until the moment it revealed itself as the whole design.

Set the two commanders side by side and the chapter's truth stands complete. Lee and Wellington led brave men with the same weapons in the same era. One lost everything attacking ground he did not choose; the other never lost, because he never fought except on ground he did. The difference was not talent, courage, or conviction. It was the seniority each man assigned to location in his decisions: for Lee, location was a detail conviction could overrule; for Wellington, location was the decision, and everything else was detail. Your capital is your army, and it is finite. Commit it where the ground multiplies it. Refuse every engagement elsewhere, and accept that you will be called, chiefly by yourself, too cautious. The account that declines bad ground is the account still intact when good ground appears.

KEYS TO THE TRUTH

STAND BESIDE A RAILWAY line as an express passes. It is with you for two seconds, a blur of steel and windows. Suppose someone asked you where it was going, what it was carrying, whether it was on time. You could only guess. Now put a different observer beside the same track. This one knows the line. He has traveled it for years. From the same two-second blur he tells you the destination and the stops remaining. He tells you where the track lets the train run flat out. He tells you where it must slow for the junctions. Most valuable of all, he tells you what it means when the brakes come on in open country where no station exists. Nothing about the train changed between the two observers. What changed is that the second one carries the map of the route. He knows where the journey began, where it ends, and every station in between. The train is not mysterious to him, because he never looks at the train alone. He looks at the train against the line.

The market is the train. Every move has a point of origin and a destination toward which it works, point A to point B. In the market these points are not metaphors. They are prices, exact and nameable. Learn to specify, in exact price, where the current journey began. Specify where price stands on the line at this moment, and where it is bound. Then the behavior in between stops being noise and becomes conduct. You know where the train should run fast: through open country, where no prior business exists to slow it. You know where it must slow: at the junctions, where heavy business was done before. And notice what has happened to the forbidden word. The previous truth banished should from your reading. Here it earns a limited parole. A should derived from a mapped route is no longer a wish. It is a schedule, a hypothesis with stations for rungs. The market has reached the first stop, or it has not. It has slowed where the map says it must, or it has not. Each arrival converts expectation into record. Just as precious, each failure speaks. A train braking hard in open country, where it has no reason to brake, is telling the practiced observer something. Something is wrong with the journey. Price stalling where the route gives it no reason to stall is the market telegraphing, early, that the destination may never be reached.

Dwell a moment on that failure signature. It is the most underrated gift location gives you. Ask what it looks like when the journey does not complete, when the train never reaches the terminus. It does not simply vanish from the rails. It slows where it should be running. It stops where there is no station. It sits in open country while the schedule dies. Every experienced commuter on board knows, long before any announcement, that something on the line has changed. Price behaves identically. A move that is going to fail almost always confesses first. It confesses in the language of location. Momentum dies in the middle of nowhere. Progress stalls at prices where no prior business justifies a pause. The journey loiters where the route says it should be swift. The trader without the map cannot hear this confession. To him, all stopping looks alike.

The trader with the map hears it instantly. He knows the one question that separates rest from wreckage: is there a station here? If there is, the pause is scheduled, and the journey is intact. If there is not, the market is braking in open country. He is already reaching for the door.

Now to the maps themselves, because you have surely collected them. Wyckoff schematics. Elliott waves. Market maker models. Volume profiles. Footprints and heat maps. Entire schools quarrel over which of these is the true chart of the market's journeys. The quarrel misses the only point that matters. Each of them is a genuine record of journeys markets really make. And every one of them is unreliable, or worse, until it is pinned to location. A schematic is a timetable. It describes the shape of a typical journey: here the quiet boarding, here the false departure, here the run at speed. What no timetable can ever tell you is which station you are standing at. A timetable read from the wrong station is more dangerous than no timetable at all. It issues precise expectations from a false premise. This is the honest explanation of a mystery every trader knows: the model that dazzled you for a month and then betrayed you. The model did not change. The first month, by luck or care, it was anchored to a precisely specified location. It had an exact origin, an exact position, an exact destination, and it performed. Then it floated free of location, and it became a horoscope: general enough to fit anything, and useful for nothing. Anchor the schematic in exact price and it becomes reliable and repeatable. Let it float, and you are reading the stars in a business that runs on rails.

The discipline, then, asks three questions, always in the same order. The order is the one the first truth taught you. Where has price come from? That means the origin of the current journey, an exact level, not a mood. Where does price stand now? On a station, or in transit between them. Only then: where is it capable of going, toward the destination the route implies? Observe the tenses, because the second truth lives inside them. The first two questions are pure record. They deal in has. Two honest observers would answer them identically from the same chart. The third is a framing of potentiality. It is a destination held on probation, awaiting confirmation stop by stop. This is what it means to say that understanding where price is, rather than where it might go, removes speculation. The trader who knows exactly where price stands on the line has replaced almost all of his guessing with reading. He has reserved his one permitted uncertainty for the destination. That is where uncertainty belongs and is paid for.

What makes a place a station? Business. A location is meaningful because the market once did decisive business there. A journey began there, or ended there, or reversed there. Heavy trade changed hands and left a boundary behind. Think of the origin of a strong departure, the terminus of an exhausted one. Think of the edges of the range where the market last agreed to disagree. These places are few. That is the uncomfortable arithmetic of the chapter. Most of the chart is not stations but track: open country through which price is merely en route. In transit, the market's wiggles carry no more meaning than the swaying of carriages. Outcomes at stations are readable, because the market must show its hand where it showed it before. Outcomes in transit are guesses, and the market charges full price for guesses. The trader's edge is not spread evenly across the chart like butter. It is concentrated at a handful of locations, and it thins toward nothing in between.

Locations are exact, and they live in named places. An opening gap, a void or inefficiency the market moved through too fast, an institutional number the size defends, a prior high or low where orders are stored: each of these is an example of where a location is found, and each offers a single exact price within it, the edge of the gap, the origin of the void, the number to the tick. That price is the location. Not the zone, the price inside it. To read a chart is to know which of these locations price is traveling toward, and to have marked the exact price it will answer at before it arrives to tell you what you would like to hear. If you cannot name that price at the moment of reading, the missing map is not a detail of your method. It is very probably the whole of the problem you have been assigning to everything else.

And if you cannot yet see the location, do not worry. The market will tell you when price has arrived at one, because a place that matters is never passed in silence. Price reacts there, and it signs there, and in that announcement the location that was invisible becomes plain. Watch where the market answers, and in time you will mark the places before price arrives rather than after.

Learn to recognize transit while you are inside it, because the tape has tells. In transit the wiggles are shapeless. Swings are small and mutual. Neither side's verdicts print. Delivery is neither committed nor refused. The candles mill rather than march. Nothing is being decided, because nobody at these prices is compelled to decide anything. The practiced eye learns to feel that vacancy in seconds. Notice the moment you are analyzing hard and concluding nothing. Stop looking deeper into the noise and look at the map instead. Nine times in ten you are parsing open country. The correct output of the analysis is the location of the next station, and the patience to meet price there.

The sea has known this division of labor for centuries. A captain crosses an ocean on his own authority. He crosses thousands of miles of deep water where precision hardly matters, because there is nothing to hit. But at the mouth of the harbor he stops and takes aboard a pilot. The pilot is a specialist who may never have crossed an ocean in his life, and the captain hands him the ship. Why? Because the pilot knows three miles of water the way the captain knows the sea. He knows every shoal, every channel, every depth at every tide. The economics of the arrangement are the economics of this chapter. Outcomes at sea are forgiving, and knowledge of the sea is general. Outcomes in the channel are decisive, and knowledge of the channel is local. The pilot is paid extravagantly for a few miles, because those are the miles where ships are lost. The market pays on the same schedule. It compensates precise local knowledge of the few places where outcomes are decided. It pays almost nothing for general opinions about the open water in between.

Every other market on earth already trades on this truth without embarrassment. The oldest cliché in commerce prices property by location, location, and location. No house-buyer finds it mysterious that identical bricks sell for triple the difference of a single street. Only traders appraise the setup, the pattern, the candle, as though these carried value in themselves. As though they were portable to any price on the chart. A setup is a house. Its worth is the ground under it. The identical structure that is wealth on one street is a write-off three blocks away.

Put one moving train in front of two careers. The first trader cannot bear to watch it go. Price is running. The movement is loud. The profit of everyone aboard is visible in real time. So he chases it across open country and swings himself aboard mid-transit, far from any platform. Sometimes he catches it cleanly. The catch is the worst thing that can happen to him, because it teaches him to keep chasing. On his average attempt he boards at speed, at a place with no structure near enough to measure against. So his risk is a number pulled from air. When the train lurches or slows in open country, he has no way to tell a breather from a breakdown. In transit the market gives no readable signal either way. He is a passenger with no map, no schedule, and no idea which stop is next. He holds a ticket he bought at full speed. The second trader consults the line, identifies the next station, and goes there ahead of the train. At the platform, everything the first trader lacks is standing still, waiting for him. Here is the exact place the journey must pause or announce its failure. Here is structure close at hand, against which risk can be measured to the tick. Here is information at its densest, because stations are precisely where the market is obliged to show its intentions. He looks slower. He is merely earlier: positioned where the market must come, rather than panting after where it has already been.

Expect the waiting to be the hardest discipline in this book. It is harder than the sequence, harder than the markers. Locations are visited rarely, and the train is always moving somewhere. Whole sessions pass in transit. The location trader therefore does nothing most of the time. He does it in a business whose every surface screams that doing nothing is losing. The quotes flicker. The feed scrolls. Others are visibly boarding. Understand the illusion precisely: motion is not opportunity. Everything in the market is moving, always. Only where it moves matters. The trader who must be involved will trade the open country. The open country is where the waiting trader's profits come from. And the train will regularly leave without you. When it does, remember what every commuter knows and every chaser forgets: there is always another train. The station remains. Missing the train costs you nothing. Chasing it across a field is how you go under the wheels.

Be clear, finally, about what a location is not, because the next corruption is already forming. A location is not a guarantee, and it is not owed a reaction. A station is where outcomes become readable, not where they become yours by right. The previous truth applies with full force at the platform. The level that breaks teaches you exactly as much as the level that holds. Provided, that is, you were watching it as a question and not defending it as a possession. When price arrives at a true location, the market must answer something. Continue or reverse, absorb or reject. Either answer is information of the highest grade. When price does the same dance in the middle of nowhere, it answers nothing, whatever the dance looks like. The location does not tell you what will happen. It tells you that what happens next will finally mean something. That is the most a trader can ever be given in advance.

GATE I · GOVERNING CYCLE & MODEL

Before the level, the cycle.

The governing cycle, on the day: accumulation, distribution, re-distribution.

THE SEQUENCE, WALKED LIVE

essentialtruthsoftrading.com/seqorder

GATE III · LOWER TIMEFRAME CYCLE

The same move, one magnification in.

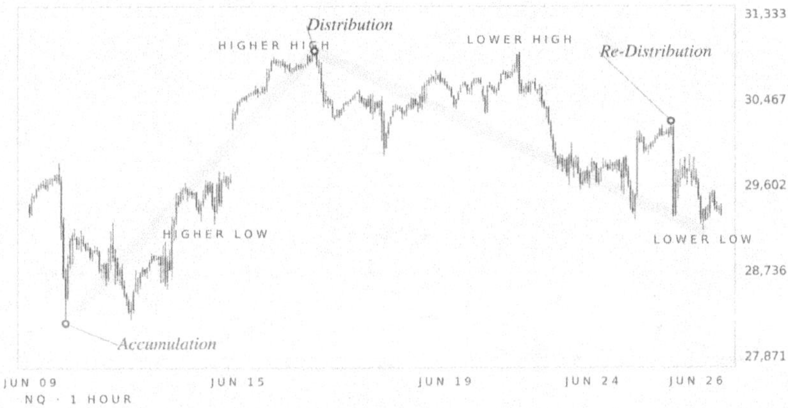

The same move, one magnification in: the hour.

THE SEQUENCE, WALKED LIVE

essentialtruthsoftrading.com/seqorder

GATE III · LOWER TIMEFRAME CYCLE

Zoom in: the cycle within the cycle.

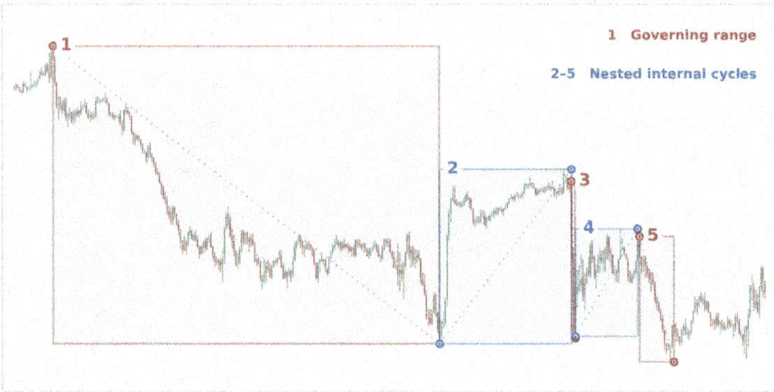

NQ · 15 MIN · JUN 22-26

Deeper still: the governing range and its nested internal cycles.

THE SEQUENCE, WALKED LIVE

essentialtruthsoftrading.com/seqorder

GATE II · LOCATION

Location on the map.

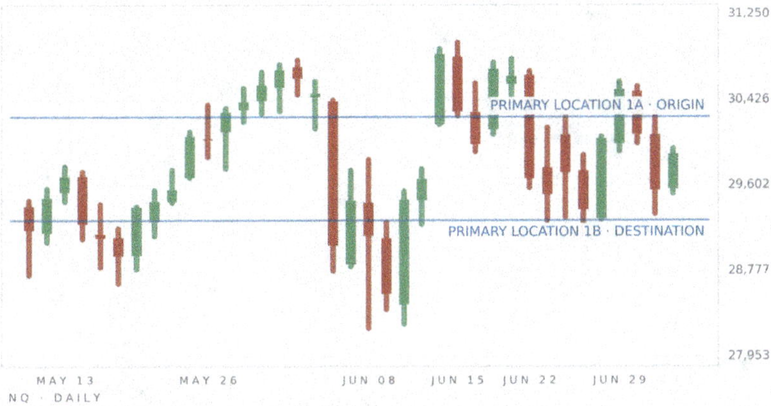

Location on the map. Origin and destination, in exact prices.

THE SEQUENCE, WALKED LIVE

essentialtruthsoftrading.com/seqorder

GATE II · LOCATION · SUB-LOCATIONS

The map, drawn down to the fifteen.

NQ · 15 MIN · JUN 22–JUL 3

The map, drawn down to the fifteen: primary locations and their sub-locations.

THE SEQUENCE, WALKED LIVE

essentialtruthsoftrading.com/seqorder

IMAGE

The Waterhole. The plain is endless, and the herds cross it all day within sight of the leopard, yet she does not chase across open ground. She walks to the water and lies down. She may wait a day, or two; the plain decides nothing, and she does not consult it. Thirst decides. Everything that lives must come to the water, and so the hunt is settled by geography before it begins. The chase in the open is the amateur's hunt: spectacular, exhausting, and usually empty. The wait at the water is the professional's: still, unhurried, and fed.

AUTHORITY

"Whoever is first in the field and awaits the coming of the enemy, will be fresh for the fight; whoever is second in the field and has to hasten to battle will arrive exhausted." — Sun Tzu, The Art of War, translated by Lionel Giles, 1910

REVERSAL

LOCATIONS DECAY, AND THE trader who forgets this converts the third truth into a superstition. A place is meaningful because of the business the market once did there, and markets migrate: the business moves, the participants change, the station closes. The level that paid you twice becomes, by the fifth defense, a shrine you are guarding on a line the express no longer serves. Never defend a location because you once profited there. The market keeps no register of your trades; it does not remember what it paid you, and it owes the place nothing. Only you remember, and your memory of the profit is not a property of the price. Every location is a claim about the market's memory, and memory fades on every timescale, so the map must be resurveyed as a discipline, not redrawn once and framed.

The opposite corruption is subtler and today far more common: the trader so enamored of location that he finds it everywhere. His chart carries forty lines in six colors, every historical wiggle promoted to a station, every station sacred. He has not mapped the line; he has buried it. A map on which every point is marked is a map of nothing, and if every price is a location, then no price is. The test from the second truth does the pruning without mercy: a true location is one that two informed observers would mark independently, the origin everyone can see, the boundary no honest eye can miss. What survives that test will fit on one hand, and it should. The power of location comes from its scarcity. Guard the scarcity, resurvey the ground, and stand only where the ground itself would be pointed to by strangers.

There remains a question the map alone cannot answer. What made the business happen at those places to begin with? Why did the market stop there, turn there, accept or refuse those prices and not others? A station, after all, is only the visible mark of an agreement: the market once found those prices worth trading heavily, and then found the surrounding prices worth leaving. The name of that agreement is value, and it is the reference from which every journey departs and against which every destination is measured. That is the fourth truth: Value.

CHAPTER 4

VALUE

Water Seeking Its Level

Value is the reference from which every movement is measured. The market is not a battlefield where buyers and sellers wage war; it is an auction forever searching for the prices where business belongs. Learn to read where value lies within the current range, and where that range sits within the range that governs it, and every entry becomes one of two honest acts: buying at a discount, or selling at a premium. Everything else is paying retail.

TRANSGRESSION OF THE TRUTH

THROUGH THE 1970s, AS inflation ate the American dollar, two sons of one of the richest men in Texas convinced themselves of a thesis that was substantially correct. Nelson Bunker Hunt and his brother William Herbert believed paper money was being debased and that silver, scarce and monetary and industrially indispensable, was absurdly underpriced. They began to buy it. They bought bullion and they bought futures, year after year, in quantities no private buyer had ever attempted, and in time, with partners from the Arabian Gulf, they came to control silver in the order of a hundred million ounces, a commanding share of everything available for delivery in the world. The price answered. Silver, around six dollars an ounce at the start of 1979, passed twenty by the autumn, thirty by the turn of the year, and in January 1980 it touched fifty dollars an ounce. On paper the brothers had made billions, and the thesis looked like the trade of the century.

But watch closely what the market was actually saying at fifty dollars, because the Hunts did not. An auction accepts a price when business continues there, when both sides keep meeting and trade keeps clearing. At fifty dollars, silver did the opposite. The world began emptying its drawers. Families melted heirloom tea sets; refiners ran around the clock on scrap; recyclers stripped silver from photographic film; mines accelerated everything they had. Tiffany, the jeweler, took out a newspaper advertisement denouncing the hoarding of silver as unconscionable. At the price the Hunts had created, the entire planet wanted to be a seller, and the only meaningful buyers left were the Hunts themselves. That is not a market accepting value. That is a price held up a slope by two pairs of hands, quoting their own bid back to them and calling it wealth.

Every arrangement that holds price away from value is temporary and expensive to maintain, and the expense now arrived. In January 1980 the exchange, alarmed at a market cornered against itself, raised margin requirements and then restricted silver futures trading to liquidation only: no new positions, sellers welcome, buyers barred. The one force holding price up the slope, fresh buying, was switched off, and price began its search for level. Silver fell for weeks, and every dollar of decline enlarged the margin calls on the mountain of contracts the brothers held.

On the twenty-seventh of March, 1980, a day the industry still calls Silver Thursday, silver traded near ten dollars, the Hunts missed a margin call of roughly one hundred million dollars, and the ensuing panic threatened their brokers, their banks, and for one afternoon the wider financial system, until a consortium loan of over a billion dollars was assembled to unwind the position in an orderly ruin. The brothers spent the following decade being dismantled: lawsuits, fines, a ban from the commodity markets, and, for Bunker Hunt, personal bankruptcy. He had been one of the richest men alive.

The bitterest detail is that the thesis was right. Inflation was real; silver had been cheap; a patient accumulation at discount would have made the family another fortune. The Hunts were not destroyed by being wrong about silver. They were destroyed by proving, at billion-dollar scale, the truth of this chapter: money can force price anywhere, and no amount of money can force the market to accept that price as value. Price without acceptance is not wealth. It is a debt to the auction, and the auction always collects.

INTERPRETATION

THE HUNTS MADE THE elemental confusion this chapter exists to cure: they mistook price for value because they had manufactured the price themselves. Every tick above the market's accepted value was not profit banked but liability accrued, a level that had to be defended with fresh money against the whole world's willingness to sell. The moment the defense paused, the market resumed its search for the last place where two-sided business had actually cleared, and it cut through their billions on the way down like water through a failed dam. What looked like the most powerful position in the history of commodities was, read correctly, the most fragile: a price with exactly two believers.

The retail trader runs the same confusion daily at smaller scale, in the opposite direction. He sees a price moving and concludes the move itself is proof of value: it is at fifty, so it must be worth fifty; it is rising, so it must be cheap at any price. He becomes the marginal buyer holding price up the slope, financing, with his stop losses, the market's inevitable trip back toward the last accepted value. The lesson of the Hunts is not about corners or margin calls. It is that acceptance, not level, is what makes a price real: business continuing, both sides meeting, trade clearing and staying. Learn to ask of any price the question the Hunts never asked of fifty-dollar silver: is anyone actually doing business here, or is this price merely visiting?

OBSERVANCE OF THE TRUTH

BENJAMIN GRAHAM ARRIVED AT the doctrine of value the honest way: he was nearly destroyed for not having it. A brilliant young money manager through the 1920s, he was carried into the crash of 1929 believing, like everyone around him, that the quoted price was a fact about worth. Between 1929 and 1932 his partnership lost roughly seventy percent of its capital, and Graham spent the rest of his life building the intellectual machinery that would make such a mistake impossible for anyone who adopted it. The machinery rests on a single separation, so simple it can be taught to a child and so profound that most professionals never truly absorb it: price is what the market says today; value is what the thing is worth; and the two are different numbers that occasionally, briefly, agree.

He taught the separation through a character. Imagine, Graham said, that you own a share in a private business alongside a partner named Mr. Market. Every day without fail, Mr. Market names a price at which he will buy your interest or sell you his. Some days his price is sensible. But the partner is a manic-depressive: on his euphoric days he quotes you absurdly high, and on his despairing days he offers you his share for a fraction of its worth. Two facts about the arrangement matter. First, you are entirely free to ignore him; he takes no offense, and returns tomorrow with a new price. Second, and this is the whole doctrine, his quote is an offer, never a verdict. It is information about his mood, not about the business. Your task is to know the value of the business yourself, and to transact with your excitable partner only when his mood misprices it: buying from his despair, selling to his euphoria, and doing nothing at all, most days, when his price and the value roughly agree.

On this foundation Graham built the margin of safety, the requirement that you act only when price is displaced from value by enough that even a flawed appraisal survives. He rebuilt his fortune with it, compounded for decades with it, wrote the two books that trained generations in it, and produced from his classroom the most celebrated investor of the following century, who summarized his teacher's chapter on Mr. Market as the most important thing ever written about investing. Graham's revenge on 1929 was not a prediction. It was a procedure: appraise value first, treat every price as a mood, and let the distance between them, and nothing else, tell you when to act.

Notice what the procedure renounces. Graham did not forecast Mr. Market's moods, argue with them, or explain them. Tomorrow's quote was none of his business. His edge did not come from knowing what price would do next; it came from always knowing where value stood, so that whatever price did next was instantly legible as gift, insult, or noise. He had turned the terrifying flicker of the tape into the babble of one melodramatic counterparty, and against a counterparty whose moods you do not share, patience is not a virtue. It is a weapon.

INTERPRETATION

THE ALLEGORY'S GENIUS IS that it relocates authority. To the untrained trader, price is a pronouncement from the market-god: it moves and he feels judged, missing out, proven wrong, summoned to act. Graham demotes price to the mood of a counterparty, and the whole emotional structure of trading inverts. A falling quote stops being punishment and becomes an offer forming. A rising quote stops being an invitation and becomes a premium being demanded. You cannot be seduced or stampeded by a number once you regard it as something quoted to you rather than something true about the world. The question is never what does the price say; it is always what does the price offer, and offers are measured against one thing only: your own independent fix on value.

Now translate the allegory to the chart, because the trader's Mr. Market quotes continuously, and his moods are drawn there in plain sight. The range is the appraisal. Its interior, where trade has clustered and cleared day after day, is the value of the business as the auction itself has established it. The extremes of the range are the manic and depressive quotes, prices offered in excitement or fear and so far unaccepted. Where price stands within the range at this moment is Mr. Market's current mood, and the trader who can read that position no longer needs anyone to tell him what the market might do. He knows what it is offering: a discount near one extreme, a premium near the other, and in the middle, most days, nothing worth answering.

KEYS TO THE TRUTH

BEGIN WITH A QUESTION that sounds elementary and is not: what is a range for? Ask most traders and they will call it indecision, consolidation, the boring stretch between the real events. A market that cannot make up its mind. This has the truth exactly backward. The range is the market making up its mind, and the record of the decision. Within its interior lie the prices where business cleared over and over. These are the prices where buyer and seller kept meeting, where the auction found agreement. That is value, written down by trade itself. At its extremes lie the prices the market auditioned and refused. Those offers found no lasting business and were sent back. A range is a completed negotiation. It is the only appraisal document the market ever publishes. This is why the reading of the current range is among the first exercises of any competent analysis. It sits near the top of the sequence the first truth demanded. Before any thought of a trade, establish where value truly lies. The range is where the market wrote it.

To read it correctly, you must first unlearn the war. The most popular story in trading casts every move as a battle. Bulls against bears, armies defending levels, breakouts as breaches in the wall, wicks as skirmishes won and lost. It is dramatic, it is everywhere, and it is false. Its falseness costs money, because a trader who sees war reads every movement as somebody winning. See instead what the movement actually is: an auction searching. An extension away from the range interior is not an offensive. It is the market advertising a price away from agreed value, to see whether new business will do trade there. A pullback is not a counterattack. It is the auction checking back whether the old price still attracts business. Has value genuinely moved, or merely been visited? Extension and pullback are one continuous act of search, the market's ceaseless movement to capture value. Nobody is fighting anybody. The market has no sides. It has only a single question, asked at every price it touches: is there business here? Where the answer is yes, it stays and builds. Where the answer is no, it leaves, in the other direction, to ask again.

The world's oldest markets have always understood this, and the newest traders refuse to. Watch a negotiation in any bazaar on earth. The seller opens at a hundred. The buyer counters at twenty. Both parties perform theatrical outrage at the other's barbarism. An observer raised on trading forums would report a violent battle between a bull and a bear. There is no battle. The two are cooperating, expertly, in the world's oldest algorithm for discovering a price. Both of them know from the first insult roughly where the handshake will land. The opening ask and the insulting counter are extensions. They are probes thrown out beyond value to establish the edges of the possible. The handshake at forty-five is the value area. Nobody believed the extremes. The extremes existed to find the middle. Read the extremes of any trading range the same way. They are not prophecies or battle lines. They are the auction's opening theater, the prices thrown out to discover where business truly belongs.

And this law does not switch off at any magnification. Drop from the yearly chart to the daily. Drop from the daily to the smallest intraday interval you can render. The same behavior repeats. Price is forever positioned somewhere within some range. It is forever rotating from its extremes back toward the prices where business clusters. It is forever probing, checking, seeking. Even in the smallest range on the fastest timeframe, price is constantly seeking a value position. Why? Because seeking value is not a strategy some participants use. It is what the market is. The doctrine of this chapter is therefore not a style, suited to one kind of trader and optional for others. It is the physics of every tick you will ever watch, on every instrument, at every scale. That is precisely why it belongs among the truths rather than among the techniques.

Here, then, is the operational core. Every trade you will ever take, however it is dressed, is one of exactly two claims. Either price stands below value, which is value from the point of buying. Or price stands above value, which is value from the point of selling. There is no third claim. And the first reading of the claim is discerned simply, without a single indicator. Read where price currently stands relative to its current range. Price in the lower reaches of the range is trading at a discount to the value the market itself established. The auction is quoting despair, and the offer favors buyers. Price in the upper reaches is trading at a premium. The auction is quoting euphoria, and the offer favors sellers. This is the trader's Mr. Market, quoting his moods in plain sight. The position of price within the range is the mood, printed. Any decision about entering the market that is not predicated on this reading is a transaction with a counterparty whose offer you never checked.

Feel the force of the corollary, because it eliminates half of most traders' activity: at fair value, there is no trade. The middle of the range is where both sides are content. Contentment pays nobody. A long taken at fair value claims no discount. A short taken there claims no premium. Either is a coin flip dressed as a decision, paying retail for pure uncertainty. Worse, the middle is mute. At the extremes the market must answer something. Acceptance or rejection, business or refusal. Either answer teaches. In the middle it answers nothing, whatever the candles do. Watch the trader who cannot stop trading the middle of ranges. He is not trading value at all. He is buying comfort, and comfort, in markets, always trades at a premium. It costs the most at exactly the moment it is worth least.

Now the refinement that separates the experienced from the merely instructed. It is the deepest idea your charts will ever show you: ranges nest. The range on which you are discerning value sits, itself, somewhere within a larger range that governs it. Within that governing structure it occupies a position of optimal value, or of none. Value lives inside value. A discount, therefore, is never absolute. It is a discount within a context that is itself cheap or dear. And the two readings do not merely add. The larger one rules. Suppose your minute-range shows a discount, but the whole range is sitting at the extreme premium of the range that governs it. You have bought cheap within dear. And dear governs. You have found the one bargain on offer at the very top of the larger auction. You have bought the local markdown at the governing peak. The inheritance runs strictly downward. The governing auction outranks the local one, always. That is why the question that precedes every entry is double-barreled, exactly as you would ask it at the screen. Where are we in our current range, relative to where we sit in the governing range? Does that combined position offer value for longs or for shorts? Only when both auctions agree that you are buying discount or selling premium does the claim beneath your trade stand on ground that can hold it.

If you want the doctrine dramatized at the scale of a lifetime, take the autumn of 1939. War had just broken out in Europe. Pessimism was not a mood but the entire visible landscape. A young investor named John Templeton borrowed ten thousand dollars. He bought every stock on the American exchanges trading under one dollar. That was more than a hundred companies, a good number of them in formal bankruptcy. He did not analyze them individually. The whole point was that he did not need to. At maximum despair, the market was quoting a discount so violent that the individual stories no longer mattered. Price had been displaced so far below any sane appraisal of value that a basket of the despised could not help but be cheap. Within a few years the stake had roughly quadrupled. Only a handful of the companies proved worthless. Mark what Templeton did not do. He did not predict the war's course, the recovery, or anything else. He read one thing: the distance between price and value at the point of maximum pessimism. And he bought the distance itself.

Step back and notice what has been assembling across these chapters, quietly, in order. The first truth gave you the sequence: fixed questions, fixed order. The second gave you the markers: has and has not, never should. The third put you on the map: origin, station, destination, and the discipline of doing nothing in transit. Now the fourth supplies the question that the map was always pointing toward. Where are we in the current range relative to the governing range? Is this position value for buying, value for selling, or the fair-priced middle where no trade exists? This is not a new technique bolted onto the previous chapters. It is the next rung of the single sequence this book has been building since its first page. You should hear it click into place. Environment, then location, then value, each question gated by the one before it. And the question of entry still waiting, properly, at the end of a line that keeps growing shorter.

Grant two traders the same instrument, the same morning, and the rarest gift in the business: a correct opinion about direction. The first buys because it is going up. Price at the moment of his conviction stands in the top of its current range. That range itself hangs in the upper reaches of the structure that governs it. Double premium. Euphoria quoted twice over. He pays it gladly, because rising price feels like confirmation and confirmation feels like safety. He has bought the most expensive prices both auctions will print that week, from Mr. Market on his most manic day. He has called the mood a fact. Then comes the rotation back toward value, the market's most routine act. It is the mere check-back the auction performs a hundred times a week. It is enough to find his stop. He is carried out of a correct idea at maximum loss, bewildered, blaming manipulation. The second trader wants the same long. She reads the double position first: current range, governing range. Seeing premium stacked on premium, she declines the invitation and waits. The waiting costs her nothing but the first trader's company. The rotation comes. Price returns through fair value and into the lower reaches of the current range while the governing structure holds. Discount within a context that supports the idea. She buys the same thesis the first trader bought, several handles cheaper. She buys it beside a range extreme that gives her a measurable line in the sand, and a failed-auction signal if the claim is wrong. Same instrument, same morning, same opinion, same direction. The entire difference between their outcomes was the question she asked and he did not: not where is it going, but what is it offering.

GATE IV · VALUE

The trade is the return to value.

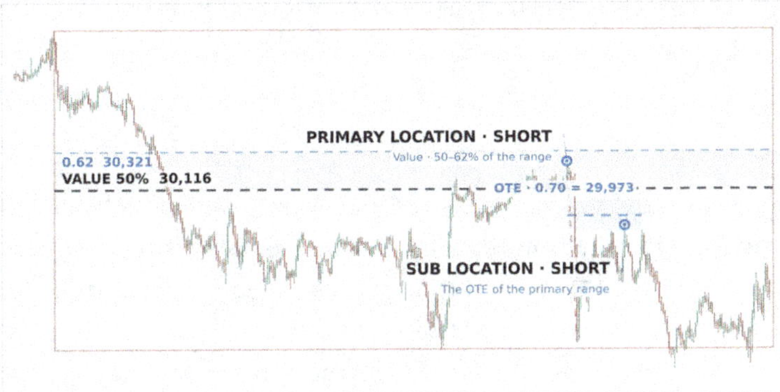

NQ · 15 MIN · JUN 22-26

Value is the fifty. The return into the governing 50–62%, and the sub-location OTE.

THE SEQUENCE, WALKED LIVE

essentialtruthsoftrading.com/seqorder

IMAGE

Water. Pour it anywhere and it begins its search for level; the splash in a cup obeys the same law as the ocean. It can be flung upward, dammed, held against a slope by force, but every arrangement that keeps water from its level is temporary and expensive to maintain, and the instant the force tires, the search resumes, indifferent to whose money built the dam. Water never argues and never battles. It seeks. The market is water. Value is level.

AUTHORITY

"What is a cynic? A man who knows the price of everything and the value of nothing." — Oscar Wilde, Lady Windermere's Fan, 1892

REVERSAL

THE DOCTRINE OF VALUE destroys its careless students by one specific route, and you must know it before you trust anything in this chapter. Price stretched away from a stationary value can be faded; that is rotation, the auction's ordinary breathing, and it is where this chapter's edge lives. But value itself moves. New information arrives, new participants come with new appraisals, and the auction picks up its business and relocates. When that happens, price leading away from the old range is not overextension; it is the removal van, and the trader who keeps selling the premium of a value area that is no longer there will be ruined by this chapter, correctly memorized and fatally misapplied. The distinction has a tell, and it is the one the Hunts' silver never produced: acceptance. A false extension visits new prices and finds no business; trade thins, the visit shortens, price falls back through its own footprints. A true migration builds: trade clusters at the new prices, ranges form where yesterday was called expensive, business stays. The moment the market constructs a new range at the wrong price, the price has stopped being wrong, and yesterday's value is just an address the auction used to live at. A trend, read rightly, is not price defying value. It is value moving house, and you do not stand in front of the van.

The second corruption is quieter: treating discount as an instruction. It is not. Discount is a state, and states are not signals; cheap can always get cheaper, as every buyer of a falling market has learned at compound interest. The position of price within its ranges licenses your attention; it does not command your entry. The second truth still governs at the extreme: the bias that price should turn at discount remains a should until the markers print, rung by rung, and the range extreme is where you ask the question, never where the answer is owed. Value tells you where the offer is worth examining and which direction the examination favors. What it can never tell you, alone, is that the moment has come, because prices are only half of every quote the market gives you. The other half is when. Ranges are built by sessions; value areas are stamped by the hours that made them; the governing range governs partly because of when it was built, and today's discount is only legible against the days that defined it. Value without the clock is a map without dates. Supplying the clock is the work of the fifth truth: Time.

CHAPTER 5

TIME

The Astronomer and the Astrologer

Nothing in the market means anything except at its time. Price tells you what is being offered; only time tells you whether the offer is serious. The clock on your platform is not decoration, and it is not a code. It is the second of the market's two objective coordinates, ruled across every chart you will ever open. Read the market's calendar as plainly as its prices, and the day organizes itself: when to expect movement, when to expect nothing, and when the train departs for value.

TRANSGRESSION OF THE TRUTH

RETURN TO A FIELD this book has visited once already, because it has one more truth to surrender. On the night of June 17, 1815, violent storms soaked the ground around the ridge of Mont-Saint-Jean, and on the morning of the 18th, Napoleon rose confident. He is reported to have told his staff over breakfast that the coming affair would be nothing more serious than the meal itself: Wellington was a bad general, the English were bad troops, and the matter would be settled by noon. But Napoleon was an artilleryman by training and by soul, and the mud offended his guns. Wet ground swallows a cannonball that should skip murderously through ranks of infantry; it mires the horse teams and slows the great batteries. And so, with the enemy in front of him and the initiative in his hand, he decided to wait for the ground to dry. The army stood down. The morning burned away. The first cannon did not speak until close to half past eleven.

Now count what those hours were worth, because Wellington was counting. The Duke's entire plan, as we saw two chapters ago, was endurance: hold the ridge until Blücher's Prussians, beaten but not destroyed two days earlier, could march to the field. That march had begun at dawn, through the same mud that delayed the French guns. Every hour Napoleon spent improving his artillery's footing was an hour of marching Prussians, tens of thousands of them, closing from the east. He knew they existed; he had detached Grouchy's thirty-three thousand men to hold them off, and, having filed the risk under a subordinate's name, he priced it at zero. By mid-afternoon the leading Prussian corps was striking his right flank at Plancenoit, forcing him to feed his reserves away from the main attack. By evening the Prussians were on the field in overwhelming strength, and the Imperial Guard made its last advance into the closing jaws of two armies.

Historians still argue about the mud, and the argument misses the essence. The attack Napoleon finally delivered was competently conceived and ferociously pressed; the dried ground did serve the guns; by the standards of everything except the clock, the delay was rational. Every variable he weighed improved with waiting, except the one he never weighed, the only one that was decaying: opportunity. The same assault launched at eight in the morning strikes an Anglo-Dutch army that must stand alone all day, and Europe reads a different century. Delivered at half past eleven, the identical, correct attack was a wrong attack, because its hour had quietly expired while the ground was drying.

This book opened with this battle as a failure of sequence: Grouchy with no order for weighing his instructions, d'Erlon marching between two fields. Stand at the same crossroads now and see the second, deeper failure folded inside the first. Napoleon accounted for terrain, for weapons, for numbers, for the enemy's character, for everything a commander can hold still and study. Time cannot be held still. It was the one resource his genius could not recover once spent, and he spent the decisive morning of his life buying a firmer footing for guns that would end the day captured. He optimized the what, and never priced the when, and the when took everything.

INTERPRETATION

THE TRANSGRESSION HAS A precise anatomy, and traders repeat it in miniature every session. The delay was locally rational: each element of the plan genuinely improved as the ground dried. What ruined it was that plans do not have qualities in the abstract; they have qualities at hours. A trade is not correct or incorrect the way an answer in arithmetic is. It is correct at its time, like an assault, like a harvest, like a joke. The entry that would have been excellent in the first hour, taken instead in the dead of the afternoon at the very same price, is a different trade wearing the same clothes: the participants who would have carried it have gone, the context that gave it meaning has dissolved, and the trader is Napoleon at half past eleven, executing a perfect plan whose hour has left without him.

Beneath that lies the deeper error: treating time as neutral background, a stage on which events occur, rather than what it actually is in any contest, a participant that works for one side. At Waterloo every passing hour worked for Wellington and against France; the field itself was pro-Prussian by afternoon. Every trade you will ever hold has the same hidden employee. Time is working for your premise or against it: a thesis that profits from patience, or one that is being eaten alive by every quiet minute in which the expected move fails to arrive. The trader who does not know which of these describes his position does not yet know what position he has. Ask of every trade what Napoleon never asked of his morning: who is being paid while I wait?

OBSERVANCE OF THE TRUTH

IN THE SPRING OF 1944, the largest amphibious operation in history waited on the coast of England, and nearly everything about it answered to human will. Divisions could be trained, fleets assembled, deceptions constructed, generals replaced. Three things answered to nobody: the moon, the tide, and the dawn. The airborne divisions needed moonlight to find their drop zones in the Norman dark. The landing craft needed a low tide at first light, so that the obstacles Rommel had sown across the beaches would stand exposed rather than waiting drowned beneath the hulls. The great naval guns needed the dawn itself. Run those three requirements against the almanac and the ocean, and the invasion of Europe reduced to a handful of admissible days each month. In June of 1944, the window was the fifth, sixth, and seventh.

The fifth was chosen, and the weather destroyed it. Gales and low cloud swept the Channel on the fourth, and the armada, some of it already at sea, was recalled. Then the meteorologists, led by an RAF group captain named James Stagg, brought Eisenhower a forecast as unglamorous as a train timetable: a brief interlude of merely tolerable weather, perhaps thirty-six hours, opening on the morning of June 6. In the early hours of June 5, in a mess room at Southwick House, Eisenhower polled his commanders, walked the length of the room in silence, and issued the least Napoleonic order of the century: OK, let's go. The next morning the storm's shoulder was still heaving the Channel, conditions were rough, adequate, and no better than that, and the landings went in through them. The German command, reading the same sky, had concluded no invasion was possible in such weather; Rommel had gone home for his wife's birthday.

The vindication arrived two weeks later, and it is the detail that completes the chapter. Had Eisenhower declined Stagg's narrow gap and waited for the next admissible window in the third week of June, the invasion fleet would have sailed directly into the worst Channel storm in four decades, the great June gale that wrecked one of the two artificial harbors the Allies had built off the beaches. The armada would have been broken on the water without a shot fired. Eisenhower knew exactly what he had escaped; he sent Stagg a note afterward thanking the gods of war that they went when they did. The gods of war, in this case, kept office hours: they were a weather chart, a tide table, and the moon.

Dwell on what the timing of D-Day was actually made of, because there is not a grain of mystique anywhere in it. The tide tables had been computed years in advance and published; any harbormaster could read them. The moonrise came from an ephemeris older than the war. The weather came from instruments, ships' reports, and trained analysis. The most consequential timing decision of the twentieth century was assembled entirely from objective, public, boring data, read by professionals who treated the sky as information rather than as omen. Armies through history had consulted astrologers before battle. Eisenhower consulted a tide table, and won.

INTERPRETATION

NOTICE THE POSTURE, BECAUSE it is the exact stance this chapter asks of you. Eisenhower did not command time, bend it, or decode it. He subordinated the plan to it. The greatest operation ever mounted was designed from the calendar outward: first the admissible windows, fixed by moon and tide and utterly beyond appeal, and only then the plans, poured into the days the clock permitted. And he refused both of the corruptions this truth attracts. He did not ignore time, forcing the landings into the gale of June 5 because the army was ready and waiting felt unbearable. And he did not mystify it, waiting for perfect conditions, for a sign, for certainty: when the objective window opened, he went, into weather that was merely adequate, because an open window with adequate conditions beats a closed one with perfect conditions every time they are offered.

Your market publishes its tide tables too. The sessions open and close at known minutes. Participation floods in and drains away on a schedule as regular as the sea: continents wake and sleep at their appointed hours, and the character of trade changes with them as surely as a harbor changes between tides. None of this is hidden, encrypted, or reserved for initiates; it is the public almanac of your profession, available to anyone who seeks it, and almost nobody reads it. Design your trading from the calendar outward, as the invasion was designed: first the admissible windows, the hours when the structures your method requires are actually built; then the plan, poured into those hours. And adopt the general's posture whole: when the window opens and conditions are adequate, go. When it is shut, no force on earth should put you on the water.

KEYS TO THE TRUTH

BEGIN WITH THE STRANGEST fact about time in trading: it is the most visible dimension on your screen and the least examined. It stares you in the eyes all day. A clock ticks in the corner of the platform. An entire axis of every chart is ruled in nothing else. Price gets libraries. Traders will study price until their eyes bleed. Time is printed just as plainly on every bar they have ever looked at, and it is treated as furniture. And when a trader finally discovers that time matters, he often swings straight from ignorance to worship, without pausing at the truth. He falls into the mystique that has grown up around time this past decade. The whisper that the market keeps secret appointments. That the clock is a cipher. That price answers to a hidden code known to a lucky few. Ignoring time and mystifying it are the same failure in different costumes. Both refuse to see time as what it is: the market's second objective coordinate, as plain, as public, and as measurable as price itself.

Run time through the second truth's test and watch it pass more cleanly than anything else on the chart. Would two informed observers record it identically? To the second. There is no debate about when the session opened. None about when it closed. None about when this candle began and ended. Time stamps every price. Neither coordinate exists without the other. That is why a chart is not a picture of price. It is a picture of price against time. Seen this way, the humblest objects on your screen reveal what they always were. A candle is a parcel of time. Its open and its close are time-markings. Its high and its low are the extremes the auction could reach within that fixed parcel. Objective markers, issued to you free of charge, one per interval, forever. A session is a larger parcel. Its open and close are time-marks the whole world shares. And the range built in a session's opening reaches frames how the market tends to deliver for the rest of the day. None of this requires interpretation to exist. It is the calendar and the ruler, married.

Hold that word, calendar, because it does the chapter's demolition work. The market's relationship to time is not a code to be cracked. It is a calendar to be read. The sessions of the world open and close at published minutes. The week begins and ends on schedule. The participation of entire continents arrives and departs at known hours. The character of the auction changes with each arrival, as predictably as a port changes with the tide. Every piece of this is public, repeating, and free, available to anyone who seeks it. And that is precisely what the mystique merchants cannot afford you to notice. They are selling maps to a city whose streets are signposted. There is no secret in the market's clock. That is not a disappointment. It is the point. A secret would be fragile, deniable, forever one revelation from worthless. A calendar is objective. And what is objective can be built into a process, tested, and kept.

The mystique will reach you anyway, dressed as insight. So you need a rule for it, and the rule is the one a courtroom would apply. You will hear, for instance, that a session's opening price must travel to some historic counterpart of itself. That this morning's open seeks an old open the way salmon seek a river. That herein lies the market's hidden intention. Perhaps. The speculation is enchanting, and enchantment is not evidence. A time construct is admissible only if it passes the tests every price marker has already passed. Two observers would record it identically. It can take its assigned place in the order of examination. It can be attached to a location. It can be expressed as value. Whatever passes is welcome, whatever its origin, because it has stopped being mystique and become a marker. Whatever fails is not a secret. It is astrology with a data feed. And the sooner you abandon it, the sooner time starts paying you instead of the men selling it.

Read the trading day, then, as the almanac it is. The open is the crowd arriving. The auction reconvenes with the whole world present. Yesterday's value is re-tested. The day's first range is built while participation is at its flood. These are the hours when moves have fuel, and when the structures your method depends on are actually constructed. Then the tide goes out. The middle of the day thins to a bazaar with no customers. This is the hour of the trap, because price still moves and the candles still print, and the untrained eye cannot see that the parliament has emptied. The market has hours when it is a full assembly and hours when it is three men in a corridor. The same vote does not mean the same thing. A move at full participation is a decision. The same move in the dead hours is a wander, and wanders reverse when the crowd returns. The third truth taught you that most of the chart is transit in space. Now add the twin. Much of the day is transit in time, and the discipline of nowhere has a schedule.

Time also completes the map you have been assembling since the train first passed. Location gave you the stations. Value gave you the appraisal: which stations the auction favors. Time supplies the timetable: when the train may actually be expected to move, and toward which station, seeking value. Departures cluster at the published hours, when participation arrives. Between them, the platform is merely a place to stand. So here is the operational question of this chapter, the one to write above your screen. What market structure must I see, objectively, for the conditions my trade requires? And at what hours are those structures actually built? Ask it, and the sequence this book has been assembling grows by its next rung, audibly. The environment. Then the location. Then the value. Now the hour and minute. Each gate opens only onto the next. And the question of entry still waits at the end, patient, where it belongs.

Now widen the lens, all the way. There is only one market on your screen. Price is the universe you are inside. The timeframe is merely the telescope you observe it through. The level of zoom is a choice of interpretation, not a property of the thing observed. It is all one, and it is all fractal. The weekly bar contains its days. The day contains its hours. The hour contains its minutes. Each magnification shows the same auction doing the same eternal things: ranging and extending, seeking and accepting, at its own scale. No timeframe is the true one, whatever its partisans insist. Each is the same universe at a different magnification. That is why the governing range of the last chapter was never anything more exotic than the same market seen through a wider lens. Your trading timeframe is a decision about attention, not a fact about the market.

The fractal truth has a practical crown, and your profession being what it is, the right word for it is legal: preponderance. Because it is all one market, the magnifications are not rivals. They are witnesses to the same case. An objective marker on the weekly. Another on the daily. A third on the hourly. Each read independently, each consistent with the same thesis. That is testimony stacking, witness upon witness, into a preponderance of objective evidence. It is the strongest position a trader can occupy, because no single frame convicted. Agreement did. Mind the standard, though, for it is strict. The witnesses must be independent. Each frame is examined on its own terms, in the fixed order the first truth demands, governing frames before local ones, before any comparing begins. Evidence is what the frames say when questioned separately. What they say when led by a trader who needs a particular answer is something else. The reversal will name it.

One more use of the clock, and it will save you real money long before the ninth truth formalizes it. Every trade you frame carries an expectation of behavior, and behavior happens in time. The premise is not merely that price will go somewhere. It is that price will begin doing certain things within a certain span. Participation arrives at the open, so the level should be defended promptly. The departure is due within the hour that fuels it. When the expected behavior does not arrive on schedule, the market is disagreeing with you, even though no price line has been touched. The market can vote against your thesis in either of its two coordinates. It can go to the wrong place. Or it can fail to leave on time. The second vote usually arrives first. Watch only the price stop and you are reading half the ballot. A thesis that is merely early is punished in interest. A thesis whose hour has passed is not early. It is wrong, and the clock announced it while price was still being polite.

One setup, printed twice with textbook fidelity, and a trader standing at each printing. The first takes it in the session's opening hours. The crowd is arriving. Participation is at its flood. The auction is actively seeking value, and the structure that produced the signal was built by that full assembly. The move has fuel. Whichever way the market answers, the answer is a decision, made by a quorum, readable and real. The second trader takes the identical print in the smallest hours of the night, in the corridor with the three men. The pattern is flawless. That is the trap of it. A setup is a sentence, and the hour is the tone of voice. The same words that are a verdict at the open are a mutter at three in the morning. Nobody who moves markets is present. His stop is found not by a decision but by a drift, a wander with no crowd behind it. He will study that chart for weeks, hunting the flaw in a pattern that had none. The flaw was the clock. A setup without a time is not a setup. It is a shape.

Nothing means anything except at its time. The sessions and their macro windows, measured.

THE SEQUENCE, WALKED LIVE

essentialtruthsoftrading.com/seqorder

IMAGE

The Astronomer and the Astrologer. Two men study the same sky. The first consults the ephemeris, tables public for three centuries, and tells you to the second when the eclipse will begin; fleets set their chronometers by his work. The second reads the same stars and sells you secrets: hidden houses, coded hours, meanings reserved for initiates, available at a price. Same sky, same stars, same clock. One deals in data and is merely right. The other deals in mystique and is merely rich, until his clients do the arithmetic. The market hangs the same sky above every trader. Choose which reader of it you will be, and choose knowing that only one of them ever predicted anything.

AUTHORITY

"To every thing there is a season, and a time to every purpose under the heaven." — Ecclesiastes 3:1, King James Version, 1611

REVERSAL

TIME, MASTERED, BREEDS ITS own transgression: the clock-worshipper, who has learned that the hour matters and concluded that the hour is enough. He trades the open because it is the open, the session because it is the session, the window because it is the window, and he has inverted Napoleon without improving on him: action at the right hour that is wrong in every other respect. Hold the doctrine with both hands. Time is a filter and a scheduler, never a trigger. The open guarantees participation; it has never once guaranteed direction. The admissible window licenses your attention, exactly as the discount licensed it in the last chapter; the markers must still print, rung by rung, has by has, before attention becomes action. Time is one witness, and no court convicts on one witness. It tells you when the question is worth asking. It cannot answer the question, and the trader who lets it is not reading the calendar anymore. He is worshipping it.

The second corruption is the fractal truth turned against its owner. Since the market offers a chart at every magnification, the trader refused by his own timeframe can always descend: the daily says no, so he consults the hourly; the hourly demurs, so he interrogates the minutes, sinking through the zoom until some frame somewhere, in some light, appears to agree with what he already wanted. He calls this multi-timeframe analysis. It is timeframe-shopping, and the legal register exposes it instantly: preponderance requires independent witnesses examined in fixed order, not a search conducted downward until testimony pleases the client. If the governing frames refuse the case, the case is refused; the minutes cannot overrule the week, any more than a corridor conversation overrules a parliament. The telescope exists to serve the eye. Spin the zoom until you see what you hoped for, and you have committed Kinnebrook's error with better equipment: the distortion is back in the instrument, and this time you installed it yourself.

And so the coordinates are complete. You hold the where of the third truth, the worth of the fourth, and now the when: the full grammar of a market that need no longer be guessed at, because everything it does is now positioned, priced, and timed. What remains is to put the grammar to work, to stop parsing the market's words one by one and begin hearing it speak in sentences: structure, location, value, and repetition assembled into meaning. The market is talking all day long to anyone equipped to listen. Learning to listen, without predicting, without projecting, without finishing its sentences for it, is the work of the sixth truth: Language.

CHAPTER 6

LANGUAGE

The Night Watchman

The market speaks all day to anyone equipped to listen. It does not prophesy; it reports. Structure, location, value, and time are its grammar. The candle is merely its alphabet. The task is never to predict what the market will say next; the task is to read, accurately and at the appointed moment, what it is saying now. Learn the difference. The first is gambling with extra steps. The second is the profession.

TRANSGRESSION OF THE TRUTH

IN THE ROME OF the mid-seventeenth century, no scholar stood higher than Athanasius Kircher. A Jesuit professor at the Collegio Romano, he wrote with authority on optics, magnetism, music, medicine, and China; he had himself lowered into the smoking crater of Vesuvius to study its workings; his museum of wonders drew visitors from across Europe, and his admirers called him the master of a hundred arts. So when the popes began raising Egypt's fallen obelisks above the piazzas of Rome, there was never a question of who would be summoned to read them. The hieroglyphs had been silent for more than a thousand years, the last men who could read them long dead, and Europe believed that if any living mind could recover the oldest writing on earth, it was Kircher's.

He never doubted it himself. Following the mystical tradition of his era, Kircher held that the hieroglyphs were not really writing at all: no grammar, no sounds, no sentences, but pure symbols, each figure a sealed capsule of priestly wisdom, to be opened one emblem at a time by a mind sufficiently stocked with ancient learning. His mind was nothing if not stocked. Across the enormous volumes of his Oedipus Aegyptiacus he published translation after translation, reading each sign as a complete mystical idea and assembling from them paragraphs of Hermetic profundity. In one notorious case, a short royal inscription that in fact records little more than a pharaoh's name and titles became, in Kircher's rendering, an elaborate meditation on the benefits of the divine Osiris, to be procured by sacred ceremonies. A name. He had turned a name into a sermon.

And he was believed. Popes funded the work; the volumes sold across Europe; the translations stood for a century and a half. Understand why the fraud, which was no conscious fraud at all, held so long: there was no living reader of the language, therefore no possible check, therefore no way for Kircher to be wrong. Every reading was as good as his confidence, and his confidence was oceanic. He died in 1680 covered in honors, having translated, by the eventual verdict of the science he unknowingly obstructed, essentially nothing correctly. The most learned man in Europe had spent thirty years writing fan fiction about a language and calling it reading.

Mark the method, because the method was the whole disaster. Kircher assigned meaning to symbols in isolation: a dictionary without a grammar. Each sign meant what it meant regardless of its neighbors, its position, its repetition, its context; and since the meaning came from his own erudition rather than from the system's behavior, more erudition produced only more elaborate error. His genius was never the obstacle to truth. His genius was the engine of the error, elaborating misreadings into architecture. What he lacked no brilliance could supply: a method that let the script itself, rather than the reader, decide what the script was saying.

INTERPRETATION

KIRCHER IS EVERY TRADER who knows what the pattern means. The hammer means reversal. The flag means continuation. The engulfing candle means the buyers have arrived. Meaning assigned to the symbol in isolation, portable to any chart, any location, any hour, exactly as Kircher's Osiris traveled from obelisk to obelisk regardless of what the stones actually said. And the error is protected by the same unfalsifiability that protected him: the trader with a dictionary of patterns and no grammar can always find, in the noise of enough outcomes, confirmations to remember and failures to forget. His readings are as good as his confidence, and confidence, in the absence of a system that can contradict it, grows without limit.

Note also what Kircher proves about intellect, since this book has proven it once already with Newton and the point cannot be overpaid: cleverness does not protect against misreading; it industrializes it. A dull trader misreads a chart and takes one bad trade. A brilliant one elaborates the misreading into a framework, defends it in essays, and teaches it to others. The defense against Kircher's fate was never going to be intelligence. It is a method by which the language itself, and not the reader's need, produces the meaning, and that method was demonstrated a hundred and forty years after his death, on the same silent script.

OBSERVANCE OF THE TRUTH

JEAN-FRANÇOIS CHAMPOLLION WAS BORN in 1790 in provincial France and was reading the classical and oriental languages while still a boy. But the preparation that mattered was stranger: years spent mastering Coptic, the language of Egypt's Christian liturgy, on the wager that it was the living descendant of whatever tongue the hieroglyphs recorded. Nobody else made that preparation, because nobody else was committed to the premise beneath it: that the hieroglyphs were not mystical emblems but an actual language, spoken by actual people, whose sounds might survive somewhere. When the Rosetta Stone, dug from the Nile delta by French soldiers, presented the same decree in three scripts, one of them readable Greek, the race to read Egypt began. Kircher's heirs approached it with dictionaries of symbols. Champollion approached it the other way entirely.

He counted. The hieroglyphic portion of the stone carried nearly three times as many signs as the Greek portion carried words, and that single, boring, objective observation demolished fourteen centuries of mysticism at a stroke: if each sign were a complete idea, the counts should roughly match; they did not; therefore the script could not be pure symbol, and something in it must spell. Then he anchored. The ovals that Egyptians drew around certain sign groups, the cartouches, sat exactly where the Greek text placed royal names: a known location for known content. From the cartouches of Ptolemy on the stone and Cleopatra on an obelisk from Philae, he cross-checked sign against sound: the letters the two names share had to appear in both ovals, in the right positions. They did.

On the fourteenth of September, 1822, copies of inscriptions from Abu Simbel reached his desk, carrying cartouches of native kings, with no Greek anywhere to help him. In one oval he saw the sun disc, which his Coptic named Ra, and beneath it signs his stone-work had taught him to sound out, and the oval read Ra-mes-ses. The system held: not just for foreign names transliterated into Egyptian, but for Egypt speaking its own tongue. The story is told that he ran through the streets to his brother's office at the Institut, cried out that he had it, and collapsed, insensible for days. Weeks later he committed the decipherment to public print, staking his name on readings any future scholar could now check, because that was the entire difference between his science and Kircher's theater: his readings could be wrong, and therefore they could be right.

Attend to the discipline underneath the triumph. Champollion never announced what a sign meant because his learning suggested it. A sign earned its meaning by behaving consistently: the same value in Ptolemy as in Cleopatra, the same value at Abu Simbel as at Philae, meaning conferred by repetition across contexts and revocable by a single failure. He read what the system permitted and left the rest illegible until it earned reading; whole stretches of Egyptian stayed dark to him for years, and he let them stay dark rather than fill them, Kircher-fashion, with himself. Fourteen centuries of silence were ended not by revelation but by counting, cross-checking, and structure. The script had been speaking all along. It was waiting for a reader who would let it say what it was saying.

INTERPRETATION

BOTH MEN FACED THE same evidence: silent signs in stone. The difference was never information, and it was never intellect. Kircher asked what does this symbol mean, and answered from his library. Champollion asked how does this system behave, and answered from the script's own conduct: its counts, its repetitions, its anchored locations, its consistency across contexts. That is the whole instruction for the chart. Stop asking what the pattern means; the question has no answer, and the traders most certain of the answer are the Kirchers. Ask instead how the structure is behaving: what has repeated, what has held, what has been swept, what the same form does at this location that it does not do elsewhere. Meaning, in markets as in scripts, is behavior confirmed across context. Everything else is Osiris.

And take his humility with his method, because they are one thing. Champollion could not read everything, said so, and published anyway; the dark stretches of the language stayed dark until the system illuminated them, and his willingness to leave them dark is precisely why his bright stretches stood. The trader fluent in market language does not read every session, every candle, every wiggle. Much of the tape will be illegible to him, and he will say so, and stand aside, and feel no shame in it. Nothing legible here is a fluent reader's sentence. Only Kirchers read everything.

KEYS TO THE TRUTH

A CENTURY BEFORE CHAMPOLLION, on the other side of the earth, a rice merchant faced the inverse problem. Not a dead language waiting to be revived, but a living one that no one had yet written down. At Dojima, in Osaka, the world's first true futures market had grown up around warehouse receipts for rice. Prices moved there daily with a violence any modern trader would recognize. Tradition holds that Munehisa Homma of Sakata, the most feared rice trader of the eighteenth century, began compressing each session's battle into a single drawable figure. Where price opened. The extremes it reached. Where it closed. Contemporaries called him the god of the markets, and his successors refined his form into the candlestick that now lights every screen on earth. However much of the tradition is legend, the insight at its core is not. Homma understood that price could not be studied until it could be written. He needed a script before he could read. The candle was never a secret or a signal. It was an alphabet: the first notation capable of containing what the market says.

The modern trader inherits that alphabet, and with it a trap the inheritance conceals. The candle is the script in which the market's language is best observed. Whole careers are devoted to mastering its letterforms, the single and combined shapes, each with its name and its lore. Some awareness of them is genuinely indispensable. Whether to pursue deep mastery of candle reading is your own prerogative, but you cannot be illiterate in the script your market writes in. The trap is mistaking the alphabet for the language. A man who memorizes a thousand words of a foreign phrasebook can name what he sees and still understand nothing said to him. Vocabulary without grammar is noise you can pronounce. So it is on the chart. The candles and their patterns are vocabulary. The structure is the syntax: the swings and their positions, the schematics of accumulation and distribution, the levels that organize price, the runs on resting orders that sweep them. And location, value, and time, the three truths behind you, are the context that decides what any sentence means. The same words mean differently in different mouths at different moments. Fire means one thing on a rifle range and another in a crowded theater. The word did not change. The place did.

Be precise about what market structure is, because the term is used loosely everywhere and it deserves better here. Structure is the auction's committed skeleton. It is the sequence of swings price has actually printed, each one a fact, created at the exact place where the auction reversed and left a record of the reversal. It is the hierarchy of those swings across the magnifications, the greater governing the lesser. And it is the events that befall them: held, swept, reclaimed, broken. None of that is opinion. It is purely objective, printed and timestamped, as much a matter of record as the prices that built it. What is not objective is careless observation. There is a right way to read structure, a wrong way, and a no way. The trader who marks his swings by impression rather than by framework is Kinnebrook at the telescope. The fault is in the eye, not in the sky, and the cure is method, not squinting. Read by its framework, structure passes the two-observer test entire. Two trained readers mark the same chart identically. And its verdicts are binary and beyond argument: the swing held or purged, the prior high survived or swept and abandoned, the delivery efficient or labored. The language of the market is objective at every level that matters, provided the reader has learned to read rather than to guess. And provided he reads at the right time, in the right order, which is where fluency turns out to be mostly discipline.

Learn the short sentences first, because the language's power is in how much its smallest verdicts say. A swing that was tested and held says: the business done here has defenders, and they answered when called. A swing that was purged and immediately reclaimed says something richer. The resting orders beneath it have been taken. The fuel is spent. The failure of price to stay below is itself the message: a door pushed open onto emptiness and swinging shut. Delivery that is efficient, one-directional, barely pausing, says the auction has no argument at these prices. Expect no business until it reaches prices where argument lives. Delivery that labors, overlapping, each push bought expensively, says argument has already begun. Someone is meeting this move. Attend closely. None of these sentences requires an indicator, a subscription, or an initiation. They are printed in every session, in the public script. And they pass the verdict test: once complete, no two honest readers dispute what was said.

For here is the difficulty your studies will not have prepared you for. The market disguises itself in noise, and it is speaking meaningfully only some of the time. Most of the session, the tape is the market talking to itself: transit chatter, the settling sounds of an auction between engagements. Try to read all of it and you will drown. And drowning, you will start hallucinating messages, because strained attention invents what it cannot find. Fluency is not constant attention. It is scheduled attention. And the schedule has already been written by the truths behind you: location is the trigger to begin reading. Price approaching a mapped station, at an hour when participation is present, with its position against value known. That is the market clearing its throat to say something that counts. That is when the watchman in you comes awake. Everywhere else, the discipline of nowhere applies to your ears as much as your capital. You are permitted to ignore the market for most of the day. The skill is not reading more. It is reading precisely where reading pays.

Understand also why the language concentrates where it does, because the reason is mechanical, not mystical. Stations are where decisions live. At the prices where decisive business was done before, positions have owners. And owners must act when those prices return: defend or abandon, add or exit. Around the swings sit the resting orders of everyone who was wrong or protected. At the value boundaries wait the participants for whom price has finally become interesting again. Between these places, almost nobody is compelled to do anything. And a market in which nobody is compelled to act has nothing to say. Speech requires a speaker with a decision to make. That is the whole secret of why the tape is legible at locations and gibberish in transit. It is why your reading discipline follows the map rather than the clock alone. The market talks where it has to make up its mind.

And when you do begin to read, read in order, because the first truth governs here as it governs everywhere. The order of reading is context before word. Never word first. Establish what the sentence is doing before you grant any single candle a meaning. The journey. The position against value. The hour. A word read first becomes an anchor. And the anchor, as you learned at the start of this book, takes the judge's chair and hears everything after it as testimony. The trader who sees the hammer first and the context second has not read a sentence. He has been captured by a word. Read the paragraph, then the sentence, then the word. By the time you reach the word, you will usually find you no longer need it. The sentence already told you what it had to say.

And when price does arrive at the place you have appointed, the reading becomes exact, and exacting. Say it plainly: a specific price, not a neighborhood. A zone is a shrug with edges. It is a way of being right in advance no matter where the market turns. The trader who deals in zones has left himself nothing that can cleanly fail. And what cannot cleanly fail can never cleanly confirm. An exact price is a claim. Suppose your map and your appraisal have named this price as the train's last stop before it returns. Then at that price, and supported by the hour, the market owes your claim its answer. And the answer has a shape: an explicit signature, written in the candles. The behavior of a terminus. Understand the word owes correctly. The market owes you the opportunity to read its answer, never the answer you want. If the signature prints, the claim is being confirmed in the only currency that counts. The sweep and rejection. The labored arrival. The failure to hold beyond. Rung upon rung, in the sequence your experience demands. And if nothing prints, if price arrives and the candles stay mute, small, efficient, passing through your terminus like an express through a country halt, then the market has answered with equal clarity. Not the last stop. Not this time. Silence at the appointed place is a complete sentence. These signatures are not reserved for the ends of journeys. The origin speaks when the train departs. The intermediate stations speak in the grammar of continuation: swings held, pullbacks that respect what they should respect. The terminus speaks in the grammar of return. The whole line talks. It talks at the stations.

One signature deserves its name here, because the worked readings later in this book will show it in action. It is the purest sentence the market speaks at a surveyed price. Call it Perfect Pricing. Price travels to the exact number your survey named. Not near it. Not through it. And it closes there, precisely, to the tick, the parcel of time ending on the very figure. When the auction does this at a mapped sub-location, it is telling you two things at once. Your map and the market's map agree. And signal time has begun. Noise does not land on exact surveyed numbers and stop. Noise wanders. The perfect close at the perfect price is the market initialing your survey. Do the work of the truths behind this one, and you will find it arriving at your numbers far too often to be coincidence.

Now the passage that settles the oldest argument your forums will ever host. The patterns you have been sold, the flags, the harmonics, the gaps, are pronounced dead and resurrected weekly. They worked. They stopped working. They never worked. The market-makers hunt them. All sides are wrong the same way. A pattern is a word, and words are neither true nor false out of context. A flag printed against the governing journey is a word shouted against the direction of the conversation. The market talks over it without noticing. When your pattern was ignored, purged, and turned into a loss, it was not because the pattern does not work. It was not time for it to work. The train was moving the other way. And you had not stopped to establish its origin, its position against value, the objective markers, the rungs on the ladder, the hour on the clock. You read a word and called it a sentence. The pattern was innocent. The sentence around it convicted you.

So stand at the screen, once, the right way, and feel the difference from the inside. You have run the sequence: environment, map, appraisal, hour. One exact price overhead is marked as terminus. The morning's participation is arriving. You are not predicting. You have written no ending. You hold a claim on probation and a place where it must answer. Price climbs toward the mark. Now, only now, you lean in and read closely. The climb is laboring. Each push overlaps the last. Progress is bought expensively. It reaches your price. It runs the swing above it, and the run does not hold: the excursion is bought back within the parcel of time that made it. The candles at the level have changed character. Reach, rejection. Reach again, rejected again. The terminus grammar your experience demanded is printing, rung by rung. You act, because the market has answered your claim in its own hand, at the appointed place, at a reading hour, in verdicts two observers could not dispute. Or run the other branch, on another morning. Price arrives at the same kind of mark and nothing changes. The candles stay small and businesslike. The swing above is taken and held. Delivery through your price is smooth as open track. You do not act. You are not disappointed. You asked a precise question and the market answered no, precisely. A no you can read is worth nearly as much as a yes. It costs you nothing, and it corrects your map. On neither morning did you predict one bar of what followed. You asked, at the appointed place and hour, and you read the answer. That is what communicating with the market means. It is the entire difference between conversation and monologue.

GATE VIII · SIGNATURE · PERFECT PRICING

The perfect close, at the exact price.

NQ · ONE MINUTE · JUN 25

The perfect close at the exact price, the market's signature at the sub-location.

THE SEQUENCE, WALKED LIVE

essentialtruthsoftrading.com/seqorder

IMAGE

The Night Watchman. Thirty years in the same building, and he no longer hears it: the pipes knocking, the stairs settling, the lift coughing in its shaft. His ear was trained by ten thousand quiet nights into perfect selective deafness, and that deafness is his skill. But let a key test the side door at three in the morning, and he is awake before he knows he is awake. The building speaks all night. The watchman reads one sentence a month, because he knows exactly where the building's voice comes from when something true is being said.

AUTHORITY

"The limits of my language mean the limits of my world." — Ludwig Wittgenstein, Tractatus Logico-Philosophicus, 1922

REVERSAL

FLUENCY BREEDS ITS OWN two failures, and the first is the reader who never answers. Every trading floor and every forum knows him: the brilliant annotator, narrating structure in real time, explaining afterward with perfect clarity why the move unfolded as it did, fluent in every truth this book contains and unable to act on any of them. Reading was never the destination; it earns its keep only in the answer it enables. Champollion did not keep the decipherment in a drawer; he put his name on it in public print, where being wrong could have ended him, and that exposure is what made the reading science rather than reverie. The market extends no credit for silent comprehension. It pays readers who transact, and the eternal analyst, however fluent, has confused the library with the exchange.

The second failure is the over-reader, and he is Kircher returned in a trading account. Having learned that the market speaks, he begins to hear it everywhere: every candle a message, every wick an intention, every quiet drift a coded accumulation. But the market is not always speaking, and most of what it emits is the settling noise of an auction between engagements; the over-reader assigns it meaning because he needs meaning, and need is the mother of every mistranslation. His tell is that his readings multiply with his boredom. Fluency includes the silence: the capacity to watch the tape for an hour and conclude, professionally and without irritation, that nothing legible has been said. The appointed places protect you here as they protect you everywhere. If you find yourself reading closely far from any station, at an empty hour, with no claim on the table, you are not reading the market anymore. You are reading yourself, and that text always says the same thing: do something.

Here the second part of this book closes, and something changes in the nature of what is asked of you. Six truths have been about perception: the sequence, the clean eye, the map, the appraisal, the clock, and now the language, and perception, for all its discipline, costs nothing but attention. You could practice everything to this point without ever risking a unit of capital. But reading obligates. The moment the market answers your claim at the appointed place, in the grammar you demanded, you face the act that perception cannot perform for you: commitment, with your own capital, on terms that must be written before the answer comes. What those terms are, what makes them binding, and why a trade without them is not a trade at all, is where the truths turn from seeing to doing. Part Three begins with Framing.

THE TRUTHS AT WORK

A SECOND READING

THE SWEEP THEY BOTH SAW

This second reading walks the reading gates of the Sequence in their order, the governing cycle and the position within it, the location, the value, the clock, and the market structure, and it stops at the moment the market signs. It watches two traders meet the same event, a low taken and given back, and it shows that the event was never the point. The reading was.

THE PICTURE IS AGAIN ordinary and again stylized, no instrument named, every price in plain points, because the lesson is the reading and not the market. A market that has spent two sessions going nowhere drifts lower into the morning and then drives down through the floor of its range, through the shelf of prior lows where every chart in the world has drawn the same line. Stops are struck in a cascade. For a few seconds the low is broken and the screens are red. Then, almost at once, price is bought back above the shelf and closes there. Two traders watched the low break. Both saw the sweep. Only one of them read it.

The first trader saw a level give way. He had drawn the shelf himself, and he knew what a broken floor means, because every primer teaches it: support that breaks becomes resistance, and the move is down. He sold the break, his stop tucked above the shelf he now called resistance, and settled in to be paid for knowing his levels. Notice the shape of his reading. He took the event at face value and supplied its meaning from memory. The low broke, therefore down. His examination ran, as it always runs, backward, from a conclusion he already owned to the single piece of evidence that would confirm it. You have met him before. He is not reading the market. He is reading his library, and the market has just turned a page he does not have.

The second trader saw the identical break and asked the identical first question the Sequence always asks first: what governs here. The higher timeframe was in accumulation, a long base built patiently beneath a ceiling, the grammar of a market being loaded and not distributed. In that grammar a drive beneath the floor is not a breakdown. It is an errand. The lows are where the last sellers keep their stops and the last frightened longs keep their exits, and a market that means to rise must first go down to collect them. The low, then, was where this errand was bound, the destination the drive had been sent to reach, the exact shelf where those orders were stored, a price he had marked to the tick long before the morning arrived to strike it. But a destination is only a candidate. It earns the name location when price reaches it and the language supports it there, market structure and the signatures of Perfect Pricing, and that support the morning had not yet given. He held the place, and he waited for the market to make it a location.

Then the appraisal, and it agreed. The sweep had carried price into the lower reaches of its own small range and into the discount of the governing range above it, cheap within cheap, the reading the fourth truth licenses a trader to act on. And the clock had its vote. The break had come in the window when participation arrives in force, the hour this market keeps its habit of reversing the overnight drift, so the timing did not argue with the location, it endorsed it. Three gates open and not one of them dissenting: the governing cycle said accumulation, the map said a stored location at a discount, the clock said now.

One gate remained, and it was the only one that could turn a reading into a trade. The market had to sign. He watched the exact price where the stops had been struck, and he watched what the candles did there. They did the one thing that speaks: they wicked through the shelf and closed back above it, the low taken and refused in a single stroke, market structure confirming what had been purged and what had held, the language printing its verdict at the exact price. He did not buy the snap back as it happened, because a reaction in flight is a hope and not a price. He waited for the close, the perfect close at the exact location, the purest form of the language, and he let it print before he did anything at all. That close, and not the break, and not the bounce, was the whole of what he had come for.

The morning settled its accounts. Price held above the reclaimed shelf, turned up, and began the markup the accumulation had been promising all along. The first trader's short, sold into the errand, was carried straight back up through his stop above the shelf, and he took the loss where he had been most certain, at the foot of the very move he had bet against. The second trader was already positioned at the location, on the close, exactly where the market was obliged to come. He looked slower. He was merely earlier. And note what neither trader needed: no forecast, no argument, no opinion about how far the markup would run. One had a level and a story about it. The other had a governing read, a stored price, a discount, a window, and a signature, five gates walked in their order and every one of them a has, not a should.

Run the same morning a hundred times and the two are no longer in the same trade. Both will always see the sweep, because the sweep is loud and the whole market is watching the same shelf. Only one will ever read it, because reading is not seeing the event. It is knowing, before the event arrives, which location it belongs to and what a signature there would mean. This reading has walked the reading gates of the Sequence and stopped, as the Sequence stops, at the moment the market signed. It has framed nothing yet. What the ordered trader does with the price he has been given, the frame he writes around it and the grave he digs beneath it, is the work of the reading that follows.

PART III

EXECUTION

CHAPTER 7

FRAMING

The Seconds

No trade exists until it is framed. Before the market can answer you, three prices must stand in writing: where you act, where the idea dies, and where its work is done, together with the conditions under which the claim is valid at all. This is not caution. It is jurisprudence. An unframed trade is a case that never states its claim: it cannot be won, because nothing was ever at issue. Frame first. Then, and only then, are you permitted to be right.

TRANSGRESSION OF THE TRUTH

IN THE LATE SUMMER of 1793, yellow fever came up from the docks of Philadelphia, then the capital of the United States, and began to empty the city. By October the dead were counted in hundreds a week; before frost ended it, the fever had killed some five thousand of the city's fifty thousand souls, and half the population, the federal government included, had fled. Among those who stayed was the most famous physician in America. Benjamin Rush had signed the Declaration of Independence, taught half the doctors in the young republic, and possessed a courage that history should not be permitted to take from him: through the whole horror he remained, visiting a hundred patients and more a day, working himself to collapse among the dying while wealthier men galloped for the countryside. Whatever else this chapter takes from Rush, it leaves him his bravery.

What it cannot leave him is his cure. Rush had become convinced that the fever demanded what he called heroic treatment: bleeding on a scale that alarmed even the bleeding-hardened doctors of his era, pints at a sitting, repeated day upon day, joined to violent mercury purges. He announced the therapy as a specific remedy and applied it with the devotion of a man saving lives. And here the chapter's machinery comes into view, because attend to how the claim was built. When patients recovered, the bleeding had saved them. When patients died, the disease had been too advanced, the treatment begun too late, or the bleeding too timid, and the lesson was to bleed earlier and harder next time. Run the structure in your mind until you feel its perfection: there was no conceivable outcome, none, that could count against the treatment. Rush had constructed, in absolute sincerity, a claim that could not lose an argument, and it proceeded to lose patients on a scale never audited, because no audit was possible. The frame forbade one.

He even supplied what he took for proof: stricken with the fever himself, he applied his own regimen and survived it, as men survive many things done to them. His critics saw the arithmetic differently. The sharpest of them, a savage English pamphleteer named William Cobbett, tabulated the mortality among Rush's patients and pronounced the doctor's method one of the great discoveries made for the depopulation of the earth. Rush sued him for libel. And in 1799, a Philadelphia jury found for the doctor, awarding damages heavy enough to help drive Cobbett back to England. Savor that verdict, because this book will not meet a purer specimen: a claim engineered so that no sickroom could ever test it was carried into the one arena where rhetoric outranks evidence, and it won there. The court vindicated what the wards could not examine. The jury found for the doctor. The disease, in its own jurisdiction, kept finding for Cobbett.

Heroic medicine outlived Rush's epidemic by decades, and history arranged its verdict on the trial with an irony no novelist would dare submit. On the fourteenth of December, 1799, the very day the Philadelphia jury returned its verdict for Dr. Rush, George Washington, suffering an infection of the throat, was bled by his attending physicians, men of the prevailing school, of perhaps five pints inside a single day, and was dead by nightfall. The wrong courtroom acquitted the medicine in the morning; the right one executed its most famous patient by evening. Rush himself died in 1813, honored from every pulpit, mourned by Adams and Jefferson together, wrong. Medicine buried his therapy only when it learned to ask, of every treatment, the one question his frame had been built never to answer: what outcome would prove this wrong?

INTERPRETATION

RUSH WAS NOT A fraud, and that is precisely the warning. He was braver than his critics and sincerer than his mourners knew, and sincerity coupled to an unfalsifiable frame produces catastrophe with a clear conscience. The structure he built is the oldest in the losing trader's repertoire: heads, my method wins; tails, the circumstances did it. The position moves favorably and the trader was right; it moves against him and the market was manipulated, the news intervened, the entry was early, and the lesson, always, is to apply the method harder. Averaging into a losing position is Rush's medicine administered to an account: the patient worsens, therefore increase the dose, and no outcome that follows can ever indict the prescription. The trader who cannot name what would prove his trade wrong has not framed a trade. He has founded a small religion with one believer and one victim, and they are the same man.

And do not slide past the libel verdict, because it carries a modern lesson with teeth. Rush won the argument. Twelve honest jurors examined his claim in the arena of rhetoric and found it sound, while in the arena of outcomes it was killing people. You can win every argument about your trading and still be wrong; you can be applauded by a forum, a following, a room full of the persuaded, and the applause settles nothing, because your claim was never triable where they sat. The market runs the only competent court, its verdicts are rendered in has and has not, and it does not admit character witnesses. Frame your trades so they can be tried there, or accept that all your winning is happening in the wrong courtroom.

OBSERVANCE OF THE TRUTH

IN NOVEMBER 1915, ALBERT Einstein completed a theory of gravity that rewrote space and time, and then did the thing that separates this chapter's observance from every confident theorist before him: he told the world exactly how to kill it. The general theory predicted that light passing the edge of the sun would be bent by its gravity, and not vaguely bent, but bent by a specific figure: one and three-quarter seconds of arc, twice the value Newton's physics allowed. The prediction created a trial with three possible verdicts, published in advance for anyone to read. No deflection, and both Newton and Einstein stood condemned. The half value, and Newton held the field. The full value, and physics had a new constitution. Nothing would be left to interpretation after the fact; the meaning of every outcome was fixed before the evidence existed. Einstein had written his own death clause into the theory, at an exact number, and then waited for the sky to rule.

The sky requires a total eclipse to be consulted, since only a darkened sun lets the stars beside it be photographed, and the next great opportunity fell on May 29, 1919. The trial's circumstances could not have been less promising for the defendant: a German-born theorist, judged months after the armistice, by British astronomers whose brothers and students had been dying opposite Germany for four years. Arthur Eddington sailed for the island of Príncipe off West Africa; a second expedition under Andrew Crommelin went to Sobral in Brazil; and through clouds, heat, and failing equipment the two teams photographed the hidden sun and the stars at its shoulder, then measured the plates against the same starfield photographed at night, hunting a displacement finer than the width of the lines their instruments drew.

On the sixth of November, 1919, the Royal Society and the Royal Astronomical Society met in joint session in London, beneath the portrait of Newton, to hear the verdict read upon Newton's law. The measured deflection matched Einstein's full value; the president of the Royal Society called it one of the highest achievements of human thought; the newspapers of the world announced by morning that light was bent and space was curved, and a Berlin professor woke up the most famous scientist alive. Skeptics would later probe the era's measurements, as skeptics should, and the decades of re-measurement that followed only tightened the result. The theory that had volunteered for execution walked out of its own trial, and it owned the century.

Set the two men of this chapter side by side and weigh what actually differed, because it was not intellect and it was not conviction; both had those in surplus. Rush's claim was built so that no outcome could ever convict it, and so no outcome could ever truly acquit it either; it merely persisted, sincerely, expensively, until medicine outgrew it. Einstein's claim named its executioner in advance, at a precision that left rhetoric nothing to do, and because it could have died on those photographic plates, its survival meant everything. One frame made a great man harmless to his own error. The other made an error impossible to hide and a triumph impossible to dispute. That is the entire difference between a superstition and a science, and it will shortly be the entire difference between a gamble and a trade.

INTERPRETATION

THE SIXTH TRUTH PLANTED the seed and here it flowers: only claims that can be wrong can be confirmed. The eclipse result mattered because the theory had genuinely risked something on it; had Einstein's followers been permitted, Rush-fashion, to reinterpret any deflection as somehow favorable, the confirmation would have confirmed nothing. Your trades obey the same law of evidence. A trade that could not have been wrong teaches you nothing when it wins; its profit is noise wearing a medal, and the confidence it breeds is Rush's confidence, unaudited and compounding. Only the framed trade, the one that stood to be executed at a named price, converts its outcome, either outcome, into knowledge. The unframed trader can trade for decades and learn nothing, because he has never once run an experiment.

Notice, too, what the frame did for the man psychologically, because it inverts everything traders assume about commitment. Naming the conditions of your own defeat feels like an invitation to it; in practice it is the only foundation conviction can safely stand on. Einstein, asked in the waiting years what he would do if the expeditions ruled against him, could afford serenity: the trial was designed, the verdict would be clean, and until then there was nothing to defend. Rush, whose claim nothing could kill, spent his energies raging at critics, suing pamphleteers, defending everywhere a position that was formally attackable nowhere. The unframed position must be defended constantly, because it is never safe; the framed position needs no defense at all, only its trial. Serenity in a trade is not a temperament. It is a property of the frame.

KEYS TO THE TRUTH

NOW BUILD THE TRADER'S frame, and let this book finally borrow openly from the profession that taught its author precision. A trade frame is a pleading. It is the statement of claim you file before the trial opens. Like any pleading that survives scrutiny, it has three parts. First comes the cause of action, the thesis. It must be stated from the market's cycle, not from your appetite. Where is this instrument in its journey? What origin authored the current move, and what position does price hold against value? What does the schematic of the cycle, whichever school's map you keep, say has been accumulated, and where is it bound? That reading, and only that reading, generates a claim worth filing. Second come the particulars, three exact prices. The price at which you act. The price at which the idea is dead. The price at which its work is done. Exact, each of them, because the sixth truth already ruled on this. A zone is a shrug, and a pleading built on shrugs is struck out. Third comes the evidence that defeats. Name it now, in advance, while your head is cool. Then, when it prints, you cannot pretend not to recognize it. File that, and you have a trade. File less, and you have what the market's court dismisses without reading. I think it goes up from here is not a claim. It is a mood with a direction.

One claim per frame, and no exceptions. Compound pleadings confuse trials. If you cannot state the single condition that kills your trade, you are not holding one trade. You are holding two, or none, braided together where neither can be tried. Say a trader is long for the breakout, and also for the value rotation, and also because the higher timeframe favors it. He has three theses sharing one position. When price returns a verdict, he cannot tell which claim was judged. The breakout failed but the rotation lives, so he holds. The rotation dies but the higher frame endures, so he holds again. The braid of claims has reconstructed Rush's frame out of individually honest parts. Every thesis is entitled to its own frame, its own three prices, its own expiry, and its own separate death. Grant each one that dignity, and no funeral is ever ambiguous.

Understand where lawful claims come from, because they cannot come from wanting one. The cycle position determines which claims are even available to file. Suppose the map says the move is in mid-delivery toward its destination. Then the continuation claim is available and the reversal claim is not, however oversold your feelings find it. Suppose price stands at a mapped terminus with the signature printing. Then the reversal claim opens for filing, and the chase-the-move claim closes. The entry price and the death price are not selected. They are read. They fall out of the cycle the way the particulars of any honest pleading fall out of the facts. Where precisely the death line belongs, behind what accumulation, beneath which authored move, is the ninth truth's entire business. The projection of the objective belongs to the eighth. The frame's work is to require all three prices to exist, in writing, before the market is asked to rule.

The writing must happen before the answer begins to arrive, and the reason is not ceremony. Medicine learned it in the generations after Rush. Modern trials register their endpoints in advance, publicly. A researcher allowed to choose his measure of success after the data exists will always find a measure by which he succeeded. The trader who frames after entry runs the same unregistered trial with the same result. Examined after the fact, every position of his turns out to be justified by something. So the frame is written down, timestamped, where it cannot be quietly revised. Darwin's reason from the second truth returns for its second shift. What is committed to the record cannot be unremembered when it becomes inconvenient. Your frame is a contract. The counterparty is the only one in your trading life with a perfect memory. It is the record itself.

Be clear that none of this is prediction. The frame is precisely the device that makes prediction unnecessary. A forecast says what will happen. A frame says what would have to happen. It states the terms for the claim to stand, for the claim to die, for the claim to expire untried. It is a map of your obligations under every outcome, not a bet on one. This is why the sixth truth's reader and the seventh truth's pleader are the same person at two desks. Reading told you what the market is saying now. The frame binds what you must do for each thing it might say next, without requiring you to know which. The unframed trader must be a prophet, and prophets in markets have short unhappy careers. The framed trader has retired from prophecy entirely. He no longer needs tomorrow's answer today. Whichever answer comes, his conduct under it was settled in writing yesterday.

A complete frame renders one of three verdicts. The third is the one missing from almost every losing trader's paperwork. Valid if: the conditions under which the claim stands and the entry may be taken. Invalid at: the price and the evidence at which the claim is dead. And otherwise: nothing. The null verdict, fully legitimate, endlessly available. Most traders' analysis carries only two branches, long or short, as though the market owed them a position every session. Their research is not inquiry but a sales document with one customer. The frame legitimizes the outcome your temperament resists. It says today's court is not in session for you. It says no claim worth filing exists. It says the answer to the day is no case. The first truth called the sequence a filter. The frame is where the filter becomes enforceable.

Now comes the clause that dissolves two of trading's oldest self-inflicted wounds in a single distinction. The frame carries two death clauses, not one, because the position and the premise are different organisms and die separately. The position dies at its stop. Suppose it dies there while the premise still stands, the cycle reading intact, the map unrevised. Then the claim survives its instance. Re-entry rights are preserved, and a fresh filing on fresh particulars is lawful and often correct. This is the difference between the revenge trade and the legitimate second attempt. One is rage re-entering. The other is an intact premise re-pleaded. But the premise can also die while the position still breathes. A governing verdict prints against you elsewhere. The structure that authored your claim is unmade. Price has not yet reached your stop. The framed trader exits there, at the premise's death, without waiting for the position's. Holding a trade whose premise has died because the stop has not yet been hit is keeping a case open after your own star witness recanted. You are paying the market rent while you do it.

Two more clauses complete the instrument. The time clause is owed to the fifth truth. Every claim carries an expiry, a session or an hour by which the market must have begun behaving as the thesis requires. The market votes in two coordinates, and it usually votes in time first. A claim the market has declined to confirm by its expiry is not early. It is void, and re-filing requires fresh evidence, not fresh hope. Then comes the addition clause. If your method adds to positions, the additions are named in the frame, at defined signatures, in defined size, before entry. Adding by design is a second pleading, pre-authorized and structural. Adding by improvisation, because the position is losing and conviction has curdled into need, is Rush at the bedside, increasing the dose as the patient sinks. If the addition is not written in the frame, it does not exist. The frame contains no improvisation clause, and never will.

And understand, finally, why the writing must exist at all, when the plan could simply live in your head. Every decision in a trade is made twice. Once at the desk, in the cool hour, with the map spread out and nothing at stake. And once in the fire, with capital bleeding or profit beckoning and the oldest circuits of your brain fully in charge. The two decision-makers share your name and almost nothing else. The first truth taught that pressure drops you onto whatever stands beneath you. The frame is where that law is put to work. A frame written in the cool hour is the desk deciding on behalf of the fire, in advance, with jurisdiction the fire cannot revoke. The trader without a written frame does not avoid deciding under pressure. He merely guarantees that the worst decision-maker he owns will cast the only vote that counts.

Hear the difference as language, because by now you can. Here is the first trader, and his pleading in full. It has been going up all week. It should break out. I am buying here. I will see how it goes. I will cut it if it starts to look bad. Read it with this book's eyes. Should is the second truth's forbidden tense, ego negotiating with the tape. Here is wherever conviction happened to peak, the third truth ignored. See how it goes means no endpoints, no expiry, the experiment unregistered. Looks bad names no verdict, so no verdict can ever arrive, and Rush walks again in size nine shoes. Now hear the second trader. The instrument has completed re-accumulation above the origin of the prior advance. The claim is continuation to the objective projected from the governing range. Entry at the named price on the printed signature. Invalid at the named price beneath the accumulation that authored the move. Void if the advance has not begun within the named session. One addition authorized at the named continuation signature. Otherwise, nothing. Every phrase is traceable to a truth, and every term is triable in the market's court. Ask the only question that matters. Which of these two men can be proven wrong? The first cannot, ever, and so he can never once be proven right. Twenty years from now he will still be seeing how it goes. The second can be executed at a single price. Therefore, and only therefore, he can be vindicated at one too. And notice, last, that only the second man can even compute how large his position should be. Size is arithmetic on the distance between entry and death, and arithmetic requires numbers to exist. Where those numbers come from is the next truth's work.

GATE VII · FRAME

Measure everything the claim asserts.

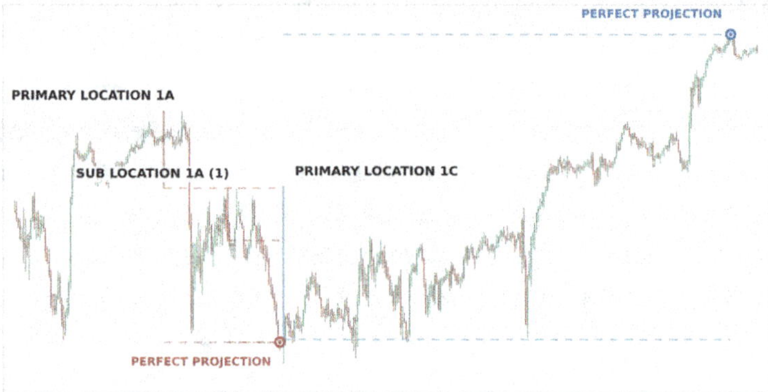

NQ · 15 MIN · PROJECTIONS

The frame, measured. Each range projected to its destination; price keeps the appointment.

THE SEQUENCE, WALKED LIVE

essentialtruthsoftrading.com/seqorder

IMAGE

The Seconds. In the dueling age, no gentleman arranged his own duel. The seconds met the day before: they chose the ground, counted the paces, fixed the hour, the signal, the count, settled every variable while heads were still cool, because both parties understood that at dawn, with a pistol raised and a heart at war, no man can be trusted to be fair, least of all to himself. By the time the principals faced each other, the duel was already decided in every respect but one, and that one was the only question the morning was permitted to answer. Frame your trades as the seconds framed the duel: everything settled the day before, so that at dawn there is nothing left to decide, only an answer to receive.

AUTHORITY

"If one does not know to which port one is sailing, no wind is favorable."
— Seneca, Letters to Lucilius, c. AD 65

REVERSAL

THE FRAME HAS A coward's corruption, and it looks like rigor from every angle but one. Conditions multiply: the trader requires his cycle read, and his signature, and four confirmations across three magnifications, and the hour, and the season, until no trade has qualified since spring, and he congratulates himself on discipline while his method quietly dies of suffocation. Understand what he has actually built. The gambler with no frame and the perfectionist with an infinite one have arrived at the same destination by opposite roads: neither is ever truly at risk of being proven wrong, one because he named no test, the other because no test can ever be reached. A frame exists to permit action under stated conditions, not to prevent action under all of them. If your frames never validate, they are not strict. They are shut, and a shut frame is not a pleading; it is a hiding place with paperwork.

The second corruption arrives after filing, and it is the deadlier because it impersonates flexibility. Before the market begins to answer, a frame may be lawfully amended: a new verdict prints somewhere, the map is resurveyed, and the claim is openly re-filed, timestamped, on the new facts. That is not weakness; that is the second truth working. But once the trial opens, once price engages the claim, every amendment becomes endpoint-moving: the stop that migrates one more swing away, the objective that extends because the move feels strong, the expiry that rolls forward because tomorrow will surely confirm. Each adjustment feels reasonable in the moment and each converts the experiment back into an opinion, because a test whose conditions move during the testing tests nothing. Hold the line with one rule, and let it be the last aphorism of the chapter: before the trial, you own the frame. Once the trial opens, the frame owns you.

The frame is the law of the trade, and it is now written. But a law is only as sound as its particulars, and the frame's particulars are three numbers that this chapter required to exist without once saying where they come from. They are not chosen, and they are certainly not desired into place. They are measured, projected from the ranges and structures the market itself has built, by methods the next truth will put in your hands. The frame is the constitution. The eighth truth supplies the arithmetic: Measurement.

CHAPTER 8

MEASUREMENT

The Plumb Line

What cannot be measured cannot be managed, and what is merely desired can never be measured. The three prices of your frame are not chosen; they are surveyed, projected from structures the market itself has built. The account has needs, and the market has never once been informed of them. Derive every number from the ground, or watch the ground correct your arithmetic at your expense. In this business, the men who measure bury the men who wish.

TRANSGRESSION OF THE TRUTH

IN 1879, FERDINAND DE Lesseps was the most celebrated builder alive, and he had earned it. Against the mockery of engineers and the doubt of governments he had driven the Suez Canal through a hundred miles of Egyptian desert, and when it opened in 1869 it remade the commerce of the world. So when a congress convened in Paris to decide how a canal should cross Panama, the Great Frenchman's opinion arrived with the weight of scripture. De Lesseps wanted what he had built before: a sea-level canal, one clean channel from ocean to ocean, no locks, no machinery, no complications. It escaped almost no one's notice, and altered almost no one's vote, that Panama was not Egypt: that the isthmus raised a spine of mountains where the desert had lain flat; that a river, the Chagres, swelled in the rains into a monster that would cross the canal's path; that the jungle killed Europeans at a rate the desert never had. A quiet engineer named Godin de Lépinay rose at that congress and proposed the alternative: dam the Chagres, raise an inland lake, lift ships over the mountains through locks. He was voted down by a hall in which few had ever seen Panama, and fewer still were engineers. The sea-level canal carried the day on the strength of one measurement: the height of de Lesseps' reputation.

The congress itself deserves a moment's autopsy, because it is the purest specimen this book will offer of numbers manufactured to dress a decision already taken. The hall voted overwhelmingly for the sea-level canal, and it was said afterward that of the men who carried the vote, barely a fifth were engineers, and scarcely one had ever stood on the isthmus whose fate they were computing. Cost estimates were presented with impressive exactness for a route whose river had never been properly gauged and whose mountains had never been adequately bored; the figures were precise, and they were parentless, numbers without a survey behind them, arithmetic performed on reputation. Lépinay, who had actually worked in the tropics and watched men die there, warned the hall in plain terms that the sea-level plan would squander lives and money on a scale France would not forgive, laid out his lake and locks, and was buried under the applause for the hero of Suez. His design would eventually carry ships across the isthmus. He would not live to see it, and history has barely learned his name.

What followed was not construction but consumption. Work began in 1881, and the isthmus began collecting the debts that no one had surveyed. The mountains gave way to the shovel far more slowly than the estimates required, and the great cut at Culebra slid back into itself with each rainy season, mudslides swallowing months of excavation at a stroke. The Chagres flooded as the river had always flooded, as anyone measuring its rises for a decade would have tabulated. And the fevers came. Yellow fever and malaria killed workers by the hundreds and then by the thousands, and the company, certain like all its era that the killers were bad air and moral weakness, measured nothing about them; it simply shipped more men into the graveyard. Estimates were revised, then revised again, always downward in candor and upward in cost. De Lesseps, who had bent a desert with willpower, kept prescribing willpower: the canal, he repeated, will be made. By 1889 the company was dead, some twenty thousand workers were dead with it, and the savings of eight hundred thousand French investors were gone. The scandal that followed shook the Republic itself: bribed deputies, bought newspapers, the hero of Suez convicted alongside his son, the verdict set aside only because too much time had passed. He died in 1894, broken, having proven at the price of a small war's casualties that the isthmus did not care who had built Suez.

INTERPRETATION

THE FAILURE WAS NEVER a shortage of numbers. De Lesseps came to Paris with figures to the franc and timetables to the season, and the congress fell silent before their exactness. That silence is the warning. A true absence of measurement announces itself: the man who has counted nothing knows he is guessing, and the knowing keeps him careful. The counterfeit is quiet, precise to the decimal, applauded for its confidence, and descended from nothing but the answer already chosen. Precision is not measurement. A measurement has a parent, the ground it was drawn from; his had only a reputation, and no reputation was ever thick enough to build a canal across. He did not lack arithmetic. He lacked a survey, and the lack was a choice. Measurement would not have spared him the cost. It would only have named the cost while he could still refuse to pay it.

OBSERVANCE OF THE TRUTH

FIFTEEN YEARS LATER THE Americans bought the wreckage, and after a first stumbling year of their own, they sent an engineer whose greatness lay in refusing to dig. John Stevens, a railroad man who had driven track through the Rockies, arrived in 1905, looked at the frantic, disorganized shoveling he had inherited, and stopped it. The digging, he said, was the least thing of all. The problem was not making a hole; it was moving what came out of the hole, and so for a year the Panama effort built almost nothing but capacity to measure and to carry: a rebuilt railroad, spoil yards, machine shops, housing, and ledgers. Every cubic yard was counted. Every unit cost was tracked. The Chagres was gauged through its floods until its violence was a curve on paper rather than an act of God.

Measurement then performed its quiet miracle at Culebra, the very cut that had eaten the French effort alive. To the Americans, the mountain was not an adversary but an inventory: so many million cubic yards, each with a cost to break and a cost to carry, each needing a destination. The rebuilt railroad ran like a conveyor, dirt trains timetabled like passenger expresses, and the spoil that had buried French excavators season after season was hauled fifty kilometers and poured, by measured trainload, into the great dam rising at Gatun. Attend to what that means: the same dirt that was the French catastrophe became the American structure, because arithmetic had assigned it a place in the design. Nothing about the mountain had changed. What changed is that someone had measured it into an asset. The obstacle and the material were always the same object, waiting for a surveyor to notice.

And the fever was measured to death. William Gorgas, an army doctor armed with the new and widely ridiculed finding that yellow fever traveled by a single species of mosquito, treated the epidemic as a surveying problem: map the breeding water, screen the houses, fumigate district by district, drain and oil the standing pools. Congressmen jeered at the money spent chasing insects. Within roughly two years, yellow fever, the butcher of the French decade, was effectively gone from the canal zone, and malaria was falling year upon year. Then, with the ground truly known, came the decision the French congress had refused: in 1906, on Stevens's advocacy, the United States Senate voted, thirty-six to thirty-one, for a lock canal, a dammed Chagres, and an inland lake to float ships over the mountains: Lépinay's rejected design, resurrected by measurement a generation after reputation had buried it. George Goethals drove the work through the Culebra slides to the end, and in August 1914 the first ship crossed the isthmus, ahead of schedule and inside the estimates. Same mountains. Same river. Same mosquitoes. Different arithmetic.

INTERPRETATION

HISTORY RARELY RUNS A controlled experiment; here it ran one. Two great powers attacked the identical problem, on the identical ground, within a single generation, and the variable that changed was not courage, resources, or engineering talent, all of which the French possessed in abundance. The variable was the direction of derivation. De Lesseps began with the answer, a sea-level channel, because desire and reputation had already chosen it, and he required the isthmus to comply; every surveyor's warning was thereafter an act of disloyalty rather than a datum. Stevens and Gorgas began with the isthmus, measured it until it confessed, and let the answer fall out of the measurements: the lake because the Chagres was quantified, the locks because the spoil arithmetic condemned the trench, the mosquito war because the vector was identified and counted. When the numbers had spoken, the right design turned out to have been available all along, spoken aloud in 1879 by a man nobody weighed. Reputation had outvoted measurement in Paris. Measurement outbuilt reputation in Panama.

Every losing trader carries a small de Lesseps: a prior success, won in different conditions, promoted into a universal method. Suez proved sand could be willed aside, so Panama's mountains were expected to obey the same biography; the trader's last winning streak proved his aggression works, so the next market, a different isthmus entirely, is expected to honor it. And every consistent trader runs a small Panama commission: conditions surveyed before commitments are made, adverse forces measured rather than moralized, and the plan derived from the ground rather than imposed on it. The chapter's application is now exact, because the seventh truth left three numbers standing in your frame with their origins unexplained. Entry, death, objective: where do the numbers come from? Not from the account's needs, not from the trader's biography, and never from the answer chosen in advance. They are surveyed. What follows is the survey.

KEYS TO THE TRUTH

BEGIN WITH THE NUMBERS that must never be consulted, because they are the sea-level canal. The account has needs. Rent is due, the month is negative, a hundred pips would repair the week. A target twice the risk would make the spreadsheet respectable. Every one of these numbers is real, urgent, and measured from precisely the wrong object. They are measurements of you, and the market has never once been informed of your circumstances. A target set at what the account needs. A stop set at what the account can bear to lose. A size set at what would make the win feel meaningful. This is de Lesseps' method, the answer first and the isthmus afterward. The isthmus will send you the same invoice it sent him, scaled to your account instead of a republic. The first discipline of measurement is a prohibition. No number in the frame may originate in your needs. The market supplies the numbers. You supply only the arithmetic.

Before any of those numbers can be surveyed, one measurement comes before them all. A frame is measured from a structure, but what proves the structure is a structure and not just a line you like the look of? Measurement. The third truth named the places where price does business, the opening gaps, the voids and inefficiencies, the balances the market built and left, the numbers it defends. What it did not say is that each of these is a claim to be tested, and the test is arithmetic. An area becomes a location only when it is measured: the gap gauged to its exact edge, the void surveyed from the price that authored it, the balance taken from boundary to boundary, the inefficiency measured for the imbalance it truly left. Measured, the zone collapses to a price. Unmeasured, it stays a zone, and a zone is a wish with a rectangle drawn round it. A location you cannot measure to the tick is a location you have not yet earned the right to trade.

And the same survey that proves the location also reads it, which is why the labor pays for itself many times over. Measure the area and its components and you learn three things the eye alone will never give you.

You learn where the purest pricing can occur, the exact tick at which a Perfect Pricing signature would have to print, because you have already marked the price it must honor. You learn whether the structure is favorable, whether the gaps and voids and balances line up with the direction the location implies or quietly argue against it. And you learn where the market stands in its own cycle, whether this is accumulation or re-accumulation, whether the last leg was a target reached or a redistribution begun, because the components measure differently in each. This is how a sub-location is read. When price arrives at one you do not ask the tape how you feel about it. You measure it, the gap, the void, the balance, the inefficiency, every element you mean to rely on, and the measurement tells you whether the train goes on to the next station or stops here. Where the numbers agree, the journey continues. Where they do not, the train is braking in open country, and no conviction will restart it. We do not guess the continuation. We measure it, and we read.

The entry, too, has a parentage worth auditing. The third truth told you where entries live, and this chapter tells you what they cost. The chasing trader's entry is measured from precisely one thing. How far has the move run without him? That is a measurement of his feelings. The surveyed entry is measured from structure. It is measured from the station, from the signature, and above all from its distance to the death line. That distance is the price of the trade in the only currency that matters. Two entries into the identical idea are not the identical trade. The one taken pressed against the authoring structure buys the full journey with a short and honest death line. The one taken three stations down the track buys the remnant of the journey. Its death line is either stretched into expense or amputated into noise. Measure every prospective entry by what it pays for its information. The nearer your entry stands to the structure that would refute it, the cheaper the market has priced your answer. Entries far from their refutation are the most expensive purchases in trading. The crowd makes them daily, precisely because they feel safest.

Where, then, do targets come from? From projection. Projection is measurement extended forward from structure the market itself has built. The market does not replicate its prior moves, but it reflects them closely, and the reflection is measurable. The completed leg projects the reach of the next. The measured move and the swing projection have served traders for a century, because they rest on that reflection. The range the market has finished building projects its extensions, at proportions any school of measurement can supply. The opening range, stamped by the session's first hours, projects the day's likely reach beyond it. A retracement framework, whichever standard one your training employs, measures where reactions have earned renewed interest. And the manipulation that so often precedes the true move supplies the finest instrument of all. The false swing is the fulcrum, and the true move is measured from it. Measure it the way a lever's throw is measured from its pivot, not from where the crowd happened to be standing. The methods differ in dress. The doctrine beneath them does not move. A target is a projection from measured structure, and its authority grows when independent instruments agree. Suppose the leg's projection, the range's extension, and the fulcrum's throw all land within touching distance of one another. Then you have what the fifth truth called a preponderance. Several witnesses, separately examined, naming the same destination. Harvest belongs where witnesses converge.

Does projecting an unreached price from structure already built sound speculative? Consider that the height of the earth itself was taken this way. Through the middle of the nineteenth century, the Great Trigonometrical Survey of India carried a lattice of triangles up the subcontinent. Each triangle was computed from measured baselines and sighted angles. Every new point was fixed from points already known. The survey's computers worked from observation stations on the plains, more than a hundred miles from the mountain. They worked the angles on a distant peak the maps called XV. In the 1850s the arithmetic returned its answer. It named the highest point on the planet. It was computed to within a whisker of the figure satellites confirm today, by men who never stood within a hundred miles of it. The story goes that the computed height came out at a suspiciously round twenty-nine thousand feet. Two feet were added so the public would not mistake precision for guesswork. No one climbed Everest to measure it. They measured it, and then, a century later, someone climbed it. You will never need to visit your target to know where it is. Stand on measured structure, work the angles, and the unreached price is as computable as the unclimbed peak.

Now comes the number the seventh truth deferred. It is size. The order in which it is calculated is the whole of its secret. Size is the last number computed, never the first. The frame supplies an entry, surveyed from the station. It supplies a death line, surveyed from the structure that authored the move, and the ninth truth will place it exactly. The distance between those two prices is therefore a measured fact about the market. Your risk unit is the fixed fraction of capital one trade is permitted to lose. It is a measured fact about you, set in the cool hour, immovable in the fire. Divide the one by the other, and size falls out as a quotient. It is arithmetic, not appetite. The amateur runs this calculation backward. He chooses the size that would make winning feel significant, then hunts for a stop his chosen size can afford. He drags the death line away from the structure and into the noise. He has inverted measurement exactly as Paris inverted it in 1879. The answer first, the survey afterward, the slide inevitable. And note what the fixed unit quietly purchases. Comparability. The first truth taught that trades examined identically become a data series. The fixed unit is the meter that makes the series legible, every outcome expressed in the same currency of risk. A hundred trades can finally be read as one experiment instead of a hundred anecdotes.

Measure the enemy as carefully as the destination. Gorgas's war was won this way, and most traders never fight it. Every setup that works still breathes against its entries. Price wanders adversely, tests patience, and draws down some measurable amount before the destination is reached. That adverse breathing has a characteristic depth, printed in the record of every prior instance the structure has produced. Survey it. Study the setup's history and measure how far its successful examples typically traveled against the entry before they went to work. That envelope is your Chagres data, the flood line of ordinary hostility. The death line the ninth truth will place must live outside that envelope, or the frame has scheduled its own destruction. A stop inside measured noise is not protection but an appointment. The trader who keeps it will report, sincerely, that his stops are always hunted. In truth they were simply built below the flood line of a river anyone could have gauged. The fever felt like fate to the French. It was arithmetic to Gorgas. Ordinary adverse motion feels like persecution to the unmeasured trader. It is a curve on paper to the surveyed one.

And the time clause of the seventh truth now collects the number it was promised. By when must the market begin behaving as the thesis requires? Not by when your patience frays, and not by some round figure chosen for its dignity. By the measured schedule of the setup itself. The prior instances of the structure you trade have a recorded tempo. How many parcels of time did they typically consume between the signature and the departure? How long did a valid claim usually sit before the market honored it? Survey that tempo, and the expiry writes itself as an envelope, exactly as the adverse excursion did. A claim still untried when the recorded schedule has run is not a patient trade. It is a measured anomaly, and anomalies are information. The clock of the fifth truth told you the market votes in time first. This chapter adds the arithmetic. You cannot recognize the vote unless you have measured what on-time looks like.

Then measure your progress by fixes, not by feelings. This is the old navigator's discipline. Dead reckoning is the running estimate of position from speed and course, and it drifts. Every hour of estimation compounds the error. That is why the navigator seizes each chance at a fix. A star, a landmark, an objective reference that resets the accumulated drift to zero. A trade managed by feel is dead reckoning with emotion at the helm, and its drift compounds by the minute. The fixes are the stations of the third truth and the rungs of the second. Price has reached the first projection or it has not. The character of the advance holds or it has broken. At each fix, the position's health is re-measured against something objective. The drift of hope always estimates in your favor, and it is corrected back to the chart.

One object remains unsurveyed, and it is the one holding the instruments. Your own execution is a terrain, and it prints data as faithfully as any chart. How often do your fills honor the frame's entry or slip beyond it? How many of your exits obey the written death line, and how many anticipate or overstay it? How frequently is the else-nothing verdict respected, and how frequently overridden? Measure it. The trader who gauges the Chagres and never gauges himself has surveyed only half the isthmus his capital must cross. The operator's flood line is the set of conditions under which his own discipline historically fails. It is knowable in exactly the same way the river's was. It shows in the record of prior seasons. This measurement belongs to a later truth in full, but it is planted here because it obeys this chapter's law like everything else. What is not measured will be estimated, and every estimate you make about yourself is generous.

So run the survey, in order, as a ritual of the cool hour. Measure the leg that authored the current structure. Take its origin, its terminus, its length. Measure the reactions against it. Take their depth, their duration, the envelope of ordinary hostility. Project the destinations. Work the leg's reflection, the range's extension, the fulcrum's throw, and mark where the projections converge. Read the entry from the station and the death line from the authoring structure, and take the distance between them. Divide the unit by the distance. Write the quotient in the frame as size. Every number in the pleading now has a pedigree. Challenged on any of them, at any hour, you can point to the structure that produced it. That is the whole test of a measured frame, and it is the same test the isthmus applied. When the ground challenged the American numbers, the numbers held, because the ground itself had issued them. When the ground challenged the French numbers, they collapsed, because the numbers had been issued by a reputation. The market will challenge every number you carry. See to their parentage.

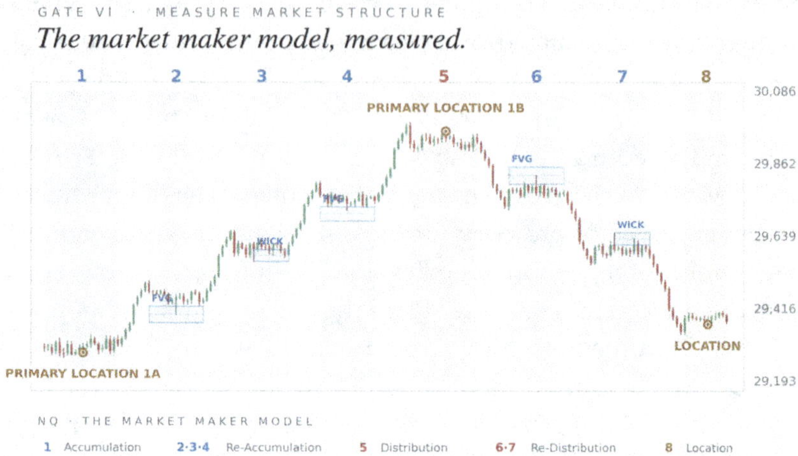

The market maker model, measured: every phase, every gap and wick, each a location.

THE SEQUENCE, WALKED LIVE

essentialtruthsoftrading.com/seqorder

IMAGE

The Plumb Line. A string and a stone: the oldest instrument on earth, and still the most incorruptible. The mason lowers it beside his wall, and the wall is judged. The string cannot be flattered, bribed, or tired out; it does not care what the mason wishes, what the client was promised, or how the course of bricks appears to a hopeful eye. It reports the vertical, or the lack of it, and every wall on earth built to the string is standing on the string's honesty. Walls built to wishes are all of them fallen. Hang the plumb line through every number in your frame, and build to the string.

AUTHORITY

"When you can measure what you are speaking about, and express it in numbers, you know something about it; but when you cannot measure it, when you cannot express it in numbers, your knowledge is of a meagre and unsatisfactory kind." — Lord Kelvin, lecture to the Institution of Civil Engineers, 1883

REVERSAL

MEASUREMENT'S FIRST CORRUPTION IS false precision, and it is the more dangerous because it photographs well. The trader with a target computed to five decimal places, from a method whose honest resolution is a handle or two, has not measured anything; he has decorated a guess, and the decoration buys a confidence the underlying survey cannot honor. Precision and accuracy are different virtues: precision is how finely the number is expressed, accuracy is how truly it was derived, and the Paris congress of 1879 voted on beautifully precise cost estimates for a route no one had accurately surveyed. Express every number no more finely than the structure that produced it: the projection zone is a zone because the witnesses converge in an area, not on an atom, and pretending otherwise merely schedules a disappointment with extra decimals. Wherever you find exquisite precision in trading, look for the missing survey underneath it.

The second corruption is subtler: the meter becoming the target. It begins innocently, with the fixed risk unit doing its proper work of comparison, and then the trader falls in love with the ratio itself: trades are stretched to promise a handsomer multiple, targets dragged past the measured projections because a bigger number flatters the spreadsheet, entries delayed past the station to shrink the denominator. The moment the measure becomes the goal, it stops measuring; the number that once described the trade now dictates it, and dictates it toward fantasy, because the market pays projections surveyed from its structure and owes nothing whatever to the elegance of your arithmetic. There is a third failure, quieter still: the eternal surveyor, who measures everything and builds nothing, cousin to the analyst of the sixth truth, resetting his instruments forever because one more measurement is always available. Remember what the survey is for. Stevens measured for a year, and then he dug.

The frame now stands with its numbers pedigreed: an entry read from the station, a target where the witnesses converge, a size that is a quotient and not a wish. One number remains, and it is the one this chapter kept deferring because it outranks the others: the death line. Where, exactly, does a trade's grave belong: behind which structure, beneath which accumulation, outside which envelope of ordinary noise? Place it wrong and no other measurement can save you; place it right and half this book's errors become impossible to commit. That placement is not a detail of measurement. It is a truth of its own, the ninth: Invalidation.

CHAPTER 9

INVALIDATION

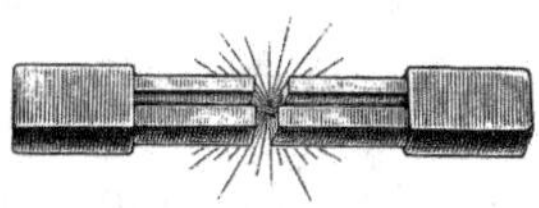

The Fuse

A stop belongs where price should not trade if your premise is intact: behind the accumulation that authored the move, beneath the swept liquidity that fueled it, outside the noise the journey ordinarily breathes. It is not a prediction of failure. It is the boundary at which the market has formally disagreed, and its placement is the most consequential measurement in trading. Dig the grave before the trade is born, and never once move it. Undug graves do not prevent death. They prevent burial, and the unburied kill the living.

TRANSGRESSION OF THE TRUTH

BARINGS WAS NOT A bank so much as a monument. Founded in 1762, it had financed Britain through the Napoleonic wars and carried the paper for the Louisiana Purchase; a French minister had once called it the sixth great power of Europe. By 1992 the sixth great power had discovered derivatives, and its bright particular star was a twenty-five-year-old settlements clerk turned trader named Nick Leeson, running the bank's futures operation in Singapore. He was profitable, celebrated, and, in the detail that would kill the institution, unsupervised in a very particular way: through a lapse that auditors would later describe with professional horror, Leeson ran both the trading desk and the back office that settled and reported the desk's trades. He executed the positions, and then he kept the books on the positions. In the courtroom language this book has learned to speak: the defendant was also the clerk of the court, recording his own verdicts.

The instrument of destruction was not a trade. It was an account. Error account 88888 was created as a parking place for small operational mistakes, the fat fingers and mismatched tickets every trading floor produces, and its first tenants were trivial: a junior's error measured in thousands of pounds. But observe precisely what such an account is, when the man who fills it also reports on it: it is a place where losses are exempted from dying. A loss carried in the open must eventually be recognized, which is to say invalidated: some boundary, a limit, an auditor, a margin call, forces the market's disagreement to be formally recorded. A loss hidden in 88888 faced no boundary at all. It could wait. And a loss that is allowed to wait does not wait quietly; it must be fed. Leeson began trading not to make money but to make back the account, selling volatility for premium to bleed the hole smaller, doubling positions so that one good swing would erase the record. Each attempt enlarged the thing it was meant to erase, and the account grew from thousands to millions to tens of millions, a compounding grave that no one was permitted to dig.

On the seventeenth of January, 1995, the market disagreed in the largest possible voice: an earthquake struck Kobe, and the Nikkei, against which Leeson had sold enormous straddles on the premise that it would stay quiet, broke violently. Here the anatomy of the transgression completes itself, because disagreement, to mean anything, requires a boundary at which it registers, and Leeson's world contained none. So he did the only thing the logic of 88888 permitted: he doubled again, buying Nikkei futures in staggering volume, one man attempting to hold up the index of the world's second-largest economy so that his hidden account might live. By late February the position was a mountain and the hole beneath it had swallowed the bank. He fled on the twenty-third of February, 1995, leaving a note that read, in full, I'm sorry. The losses came to eight hundred and twenty-seven million pounds, roughly twice the capital of the bank. Barings, two hundred and thirty-three years old, financier of empires, was sold to a Dutch group the following week for one pound.

And London paid for the grave to stay undug. Through the final year, Barings' head office wired hundreds of millions of pounds to Singapore to meet the margin calls on positions it believed were hedged and profitable, funding at ruinous scale the very hole that was consuming it, because the star's reported profits were the basis of the bonus pool and nobody is paid to autopsy a golden goose. Auditors queried; explanations were accepted. A receivable was invented; it was believed. At every checkpoint where the boundary might have been enforced, the people whose fees, careers, and bonuses flowed from the star's continued brilliance chose brilliance over verification. Your own account has the same staff. Hope draws a salary from every open position; ego is paid in the currency of not-being-wrong; the month's profit figure lobbies hard for one more day. Every incentive at your desk except one votes to keep the loss alive, which is why the one incumbent that cannot be lobbied, the resting stop at the structural grave, must hold the office.

Now perform the autopsy properly, because the popular verdict, rogue trader, is a way of learning nothing. Barings did not die of bad trades. Every institution and every trader alive produces bad trades continuously; they are the operating exhaust of the business. Barings died because one man held the power to declare his losing positions not-yet-wrong, indefinitely, and exercised it. The 88888 account was an un-invalidation machine: a mechanism by which the market's disagreement, delivered daily in the only language it speaks, was prevented from ever becoming a verdict. And before the moral distance comforts you, observe the machine's portable version. Every trader who moves a stop away from an advancing price has built a small 88888: a place where the market's disagreement is deferred by the one person with the most interest in deferring it. The scale was institutional. The physics are in your platform.

INTERPRETATION

THE LESSON IS STRUCTURAL, and it is the reason this chapter insists the death line be dug before entry and placed beyond your own reach. Leeson was not a monster; he was a man in an architecture that let the interested party keep the books, and every retail trader occupies that architecture by default: you are your own front office, back office, and auditor. The mental stop, the level you have decided upon but not placed, is self-audited bookkeeping, and it will survive exactly until the first evening it is inconvenient. The stop placed in the market, at the structural grave, at entry, is the separation of powers your one-man institution requires: it takes the verdict out of the defendant's hands. The seventh truth taught that once the trial opens, the frame owns you. This is the mechanism: the frame can only own what you have surrendered to it in writing, at a price, in advance.

And mark the economics of the unburied loss, because they explain half the ruined accounts in history. A loss that cannot die must be fed: fed with margin, with doubled size, with sold volatility, with the account's remaining health, and above all with the trader's talent, which is conscripted entirely into the service of the hole. From the day the first loss was hidden, Leeson never really traded again; he serviced a debt with other people's capital and his own considerable gifts, and the debt spent everything. You do not own an unbounded loss. It owns you, and it hires your skill, your discipline, and your remaining capital to feed itself. Invalidation is how you refuse the employment.

OBSERVANCE OF THE TRUTH

IN THE SUMMER OF 1992, the largest trade of the century was assembled not around a prediction but around a boundary, and the boundary had been published by the victim. Britain had bound sterling into Europe's exchange rate mechanism, committing the Bank of England to hold the pound inside a narrow band against the German mark, with a floor near 2.78. The commitment had curdled into a contradiction: reunified Germany's central bank held rates high to smother inflation, while recession-bound Britain needed cheap money desperately, and the peg forced Britain to strangle its own economy to defend a number. Stanley Druckenmiller, running George Soros's Quantum fund, read the contradiction and saw what this book has taught you to see: a defended line whose defenders were economically forbidden to keep defending it.

But the genius of the position was not the thesis; half the market held the thesis. The genius was the frame, because the ERM band did something almost unheard of: it published the trade's invalidation in advance, officially, in the newspaper. If Britain defended the floor successfully, sterling could scarcely rise above its band; the short seller's loss was confined to a sliver of spread and carry. If the floor broke, the pound would fall by whatever gravity demanded, which proved to be a devaluation in double digits. Here was the eighth truth's arithmetic at sovereign scale: a death line adjacent and official, a projection vast, and therefore a quotient, a size, that beggared belief. When Druckenmiller presented the idea, Soros's reported answer has entered the folklore of the business: such asymmetry did not deserve a position, it deserved the jugular. Quantum built a short position against sterling reported near ten billion dollars, a size that looks like recklessness and was in fact its exact opposite: the largest position of the age was permitted by the smallest honest distance to being provably wrong.

On the sixteenth of September, 1992, Britain defended its line the way de Lesseps had defended his: with escalating force and no stated point of surrender. The Bank of England spent billions of reserves buying its own currency before breakfast. Base rates were raised from ten percent to twelve, and then, in an announcement that reeked of panic by mid-afternoon, to fifteen, a level that would have flattened what remained of the British economy had anyone believed it would stand. Nobody believed it. By evening the government had capitulated, sterling was ejected from the mechanism and fell through its floor, and the day entered British history as Black Wednesday. Quantum's profit was reported above a billion dollars. Britain's Treasury, by its own later accounting, had spent billions defending a boundary it always, eventually, had to concede.

See the story whole, because its two lessons are usually told as one. Within the most famous speculation of the century sit both of this chapter's characters. Soros and Druckenmiller are the observance: enormous exposure, total conviction, and underneath it a near, known, official price at which they were wrong and would have paid a bounded, budgeted fee to learn it. And the British government is the transgression, running Leeson's logic with public money: a position defended because it had been declared, a line held with escalating doses because no point of surrender had ever been framed, we will do whatever it takes as a slogan where a death line should have been. The market performed the invalidation the Treasury refused to specify, and charged accordingly, because the market always conducts the funeral of the unframed, and it bills for the service at its own rates.

INTERPRETATION

STRIP THE TWO PARTIES to their structures and they differ in exactly one particular. Both were enormous. Both were leveraged. Both were certain. One knew the price at which it was wrong; the other had a commitment. That single difference decided who ended the day a billion richer and who spent the autumn explaining itself to Parliament, and it is worth saying with force: the trade remembered as history's boldest gamble was, structurally, one of the most conservative positions ever taken, because its maximum cost was small, known, and accepted in advance. Boldness in size and caution in frame are not opposites. They are the same discipline viewed from two sides, and neither survives without the other.

This is the emotional inversion the chapter needs you to carry out of it: aggression is a property of invalidation. The eighth truth made size a quotient, the risk unit divided by the distance to death; watch what follows. The nearer and truer the death line, the larger the position the same unit affords, which means the boldest traders are necessarily the best buriers, and the timid are timid precisely because their graves are vague. The trader who cannot say where he is wrong takes small, anxious positions and defends them emotionally, bleeding conviction into a void. The trader who knows the exact price of his error to the tick can be, in Soros's folklore, a pig, because the trough has walls. Courage at size is not a temperament, any more than serenity was in the seventh truth. It is architecture.

KEYS TO THE TRUTH

BEGIN WITH THE PROHIBITION, which by now you can write yourself. The stop set at a dollar figure, a round number of pips, a percentage of the account. The distance that keeps the loss comfortable. Every one of these is a measurement of you. The eighth truth already ruled on numbers with that parentage. The market does not know your pain threshold. It cannot trade around what it has never been told. There is exactly one honest question, and the whole chapter lives inside it: where should price not trade if my premise is true? The premise is the claim your frame filed. It says a campaign accumulated here and is bound for there. Somewhere beneath that claim is a price whose printing would not merely bruise the idea but unsay it. That price is where the trade's grave belongs. No other consideration on earth gets a vote.

Now the anatomy of the true grave. State it for the long side and mirror it exactly for the short. Your claim rests on an accumulation, the place where the campaign truly loaded. That place is marked in the record by verdicts you learned to read in the sixth truth. There is, most often, the purged liquidity. That is the sweep below the prior swing that collected the resting orders and supplied the fuel. The false move before the true one. There is the pivot that formed at the level: the structural swing born there, a two-observer fact. And there is the authoring candle. That is the parcel of time in which the flow visibly turned. It is the candle that created the move your claim rides, read against the candle before it. Beneath that assembly, and only beneath it, lies the price that unsays everything. Consider what the market returning there would mean. The sweep was not a sweep but a beginning. The pivot did not hold. The authoring flow has been fully repudiated at its origin. If price trades there, you have not suffered bad luck within a valid campaign. There is no campaign. The re-accumulation you pleaded never existed. The only honest response to a premise that never existed is to be gone. Gone automatically, at a price fixed back when you could still be trusted.

Mirror the anatomy for the short side. The doctrine is symmetric. Most trading education is not. The short claim rests on a distribution: the region where the campaign truly unloaded. It is marked by the same verdicts inverted. The liquidity purged above, the sweep through the prior high that collected the buy stops and emptied the fuel. The pivot born at the level, the swing high created where supply took control. The authoring candle in which the flow turned down, read against its predecessor. Above that assembly lies the price that unsays the short. Suppose the market can trade back through the origin of the markdown. Suppose it absorbs what was distributed and holds beyond the swept high. Then distribution never happened. Your claim was a misreading of accumulation in progress. The grave for a short lives above the true redistribution. Every consideration of this chapter applies with the signs reversed: the noise envelope, the premise clause, the prohibition on comfort-derived distances. The discipline is identical.

Understand why the grave belongs there and nowhere nearer. The temptation nearer is dressed as prudence. Everything between your entry and that structure is territory the market may lawfully visit while still agreeing with you. That is the ordinary adverse breathing whose envelope the eighth truth taught you to measure. The retest, the shakeout of the impatient. A stop inside that territory is not protection. It is an appointment with routine hostility. The trader who keeps setting it will keep reporting that his stops are hunted. What actually happened is simpler. He built his grave inside the flood line of a river whose rises were on record. And everything beyond the structure is territory that unsays the thesis. Every tick traded there is rent paid on a corpse. The death line is the frontier between those two countries: the first price whose printing would force an honest man to change his mind. Nearer is noise. Farther is denial. There is only one honest distance. The market dictates it, not your comfort.

Sometimes the survey returns an answer traders refuse to hear: there is no honest grave within reach. Perhaps the structure that would unsay the idea lies so far from any available entry that the quotient collapses. Perhaps the origin is so distant and muddled that no price cleanly refutes anything. Understand what the market has just told you. It is not saying the stop must be improvised somewhere closer. It is saying this idea, here, now, is ineligible for trial. A claim with no identifiable death line is not a trade awaiting a stop. It is an opinion. Opinions are not tradeable instruments, whatever conviction they carry. The absence of a readable invalidation is itself a verdict. The else-nothing clause of the seventh truth exists precisely to receive it. Some of the most expensive positions in any losing year were ideas that should have been disqualified at this checkpoint. Instead they were fitted with a stop the way a corpse is fitted with a suit. For appearances, changing nothing.

Grasp also what the placed stop is not. Half its power is psychological, and it arrives only when this is understood. Placing the death line is not expecting to visit it. The seconds pacing out the dueling ground did not expect both men to die. The stop converts the market's disagreement from a feeling into an event. Without it, disagreement arrives as an atmosphere. The position feels heavy. The tape feels wrong. Doubt seeps in at the speed of mood. The trader oscillates between panic and denial with nothing to arbitrate. With it, disagreement has an address. Until the address prints, the claim stands, and the noise is only noise, however it feels. When the address prints, the claim is dead, however that feels. The second truth's grammar reaches its final form here: the stop is where has replaces should forever. You have delegated the verdict to a price. Prices, unlike traders at two in the morning, cannot be argued with.

The seventh truth's second death clause now receives its mechanics. The premise can die before the position does, and the fluent trader buries it there. The claim rests on more than its origin. It rests on a governing structure, a character, a schedule. Sometimes a governing verdict prints against you elsewhere. The swing that framed the whole campaign purges in the wrong direction. The delivery character breaks in the manner the next truth will teach you to read. The expiry of the eighth truth's measured schedule lapses with nothing begun. Then the premise is dead while price still breathes above the stop. Exit there. Exiting at premise-death is burial with dignity. It means a smaller loss, a cleaner ledger, and a mind released for the next claim. Waiting for the stop once the premise is gone is not discipline. It is paying full rent on a condemned building because the demolition date is printed on the lease.

Re-entry, promised by the seventh truth, now gets its law. The space between persistence and Martingale is exactly one frame wide. The stopped trade whose premise survived may be re-pleaded. The great campaigns are often caught on the second filing. The first was shaken out by a purge that deepened the very structure the new claim stands on. But lawful re-entry has conditions, and each exists to keep Monte Carlo out of the courtroom. The premise must be re-verified, not presumed. Resurvey the map, and confirm the cycle position intact. The new claim requires fresh particulars. It needs a fresh signature at the location, not the memory of the old one. Size is governed by the same quotient. Never enlarge it to reclaim what the first attempt spent. Recovering losses is not a cause of action. And the attempts are counted, with the count written into the standing process. A premise that keeps being stopped is being told something by the only witness that matters. Persistence re-files a claim on new evidence. Revenge re-files a grudge on old conviction. The paperwork looks identical at a distance. That is why the frame, not the feeling, must be the thing that distinguishes them.

Now the accounting. Invalidation rewrites your ledger's moral categories. The stopped trade that followed its frame is not a failure. It is the process functioning, an experiment that returned its answer at its budgeted cost. The first truth told you a breach of order is an error whatever the outcome. Here is the mirror it implied: obedience is not an error whatever the outcome. Your losses divide into two species that your bookkeeping must never blend. Tuition is the framed loss, taken at the structural grave or at premise-death, at the size the quotient dictated. It purchased information. Across the series it is simply the cost column of a profitable business. Leakage is everything else: the widened stop, the phantom exit, the unframed entry's unbounded bleed. A trading career can carry tuition indefinitely. It cannot carry leakage for long. The ninth truth's ledger exists to make the two unmistakable, trade by trade, in writing.

Seen from the right altitude, the stop is not a defense at all. It is the purchase that makes every other number real. An unframed position carries, in the fine print nobody reads, an unlimited liability. Its true cost is unknowable. Therefore its size is meaningless, its projection is unpriced, and its place in any series is fiction. One unbounded loss re-prices the whole ledger. The death line converts that open liability into a premium. That premium is a known, budgeted, maximum cost of asking the market a question. This is the quiet reason the eighth truth could speak of trades as experiments and series as data. Experiments have costs, not exposures. You are always paying for information in this business. The framed trader pays a defined premium and owns the answer either way. The unframed trader pays an undefined premium and owns, at the end, only the exposure. Between those two purchasing arrangements lies the entire distance between Barings and Quantum.

One movement of the death line is lawful, and only one: forward, behind the journey, in the direction of the trade. The campaign advances and prints new verdicts. New pivots are born, new liquidity is spent, new stations are reached. The structure that would unsay the remaining claim advances with it. The grave may be moved up behind each rung the second truth's ladder confirms. This is trailing by structure, and it is measurement. Trailing by feeling is the same corruption in the opposite direction. That means tightening because you are nervous, or because the profit has become precious. But backward, never. Not once, not by a tick. You now know the reason in institutional terms. The trader who widens a stop has reopened account 88888 and made himself its clerk. He defers the market's verdict because he holds the books. A stop that can widen is not a stop. It is a negotiation, and you are losing it.

Close the Keys with the autopsy. The dead teach best, and most traders bury their losses without an inquest. Take any stopped trade from your record. Put five questions to the corpse, each answerable in the grammar of verdicts. Was the death line structural, derived from the accumulation, the purge, the authoring candle, or was it a measurement of comfort? Did it live outside the measured envelope of ordinary hostility, or inside it, keeping an appointment? Was it honored to the tick, or negotiated? Did the premise die before the stop, and was it buried there, or was rent paid on the corpse? And did the entry's distance to the grave justify the size, by arithmetic and not by appetite? Five questions, five verdicts. The trade's death becomes tuition twice over: once in the market, once on the table. An unexamined loss costs its full price and teaches nothing. The examined loss is the cheapest education this business sells.

The frame and its grave. Delivered to target, or stopped where the signature is lost.

THE SEQUENCE, WALKED LIVE

essentialtruthsoftrading.com/seqorder

IMAGE

The Fuse. In the wall of every house sits the humblest component in the building: a sliver of metal engineered to die. It is rated with precision, not to the homeowner's optimism but to what the circuit can actually carry, and when the surge comes it fails first, instantly, by design, so that the wiring does not cook and the house does not burn. No one mourns a blown fuse. No one calls the fuse a failure; the fuse dying is the system working. And the householder who wearies of replacing fuses and bridges the gap with a copper coin will be identified later, by the fire investigators, as the cause. Your stop is the fuse: cheap, sacrificial, precisely rated to the structure. Let it die its designed death, every time, and the house stands.

AUTHORITY

"Learn how to take your losses quickly and cleanly. Don't try to buy at the bottom and sell at the top. This can't be done—except by liars." — Bernard Baruch, Baruch: My Own Story, 1957

REVERSAL

THE FIRST CORRUPTION INVERTS the chapter without violating a word of it: the stop placed too near, inside the measured breathing of the very structure that makes the trade valid. This trader has read everything and understood the arithmetic too well: he wants the tight death line because the eighth truth's quotient rewards it with size, and so he inches the grave toward the entry until the numbers flatter him, and ordinary noise executes him with metronomic regularity. He is being wrong about being wrong: the prices taking him out prove nothing about his premise, and he is paying full tuition for lessons that contain no information. Hold the discipline in both hands: the death line lives where the structure says, and if that honest distance makes the size too small or the trade too expensive, the answer is a smaller position or no position. The grave does not move toward the living to suit the budget. The budget defers to the grave, or the funeral comes early and often.

The second corruption wears the mask of prudence so convincingly that most traders never unmask it: the phantom invalidation, the exit taken before any death line printed, because the position felt wrong. No structure broke; no verdict printed; the premise stood unrefuted; the trader simply suffered, and paid to stop suffering, and then watched the claim he abandoned complete its journey without him. Understand what actually happened: the market never disagreed with him. He disagreed with himself, over-read his own discomfort as evidence in the sixth truth's forbidden style, and executed a verdict no court had issued. The frame protects in both directions, and the second direction is the one nobody teaches: it forbids you to stay past death, and it forbids you to die before it. Between entry and the death line, with the premise intact, your instructions are to sit still and let the experiment run. Anything else is the fuse unscrewing itself at the first flicker of the lights.

And do not mistake the grave-digging for pessimism, because it is the most optimistic act in the profession: only the trader who knows exactly where death lives can afford to live at full size. What remains, once single trades can die cleanly, is to notice what their deaths and lives have in common, because no verdict stands alone. The market that killed your claim did it in a particular manner, and the market that honors your claims honors them in a particular manner too, and manner, it turns out, persists. One trade's outcome is noise. The market's habits are signal, and reading them is the tenth truth: Repetition.

THE TRUTHS AT WORK

A THIRD READING

THE TRADE THEY ONLY SEEMED TO SHARE

This third reading takes what looks like one trade and shows it was always two. Where the last reading stopped, a trade stood located and signed, the sweep reclaimed and the perfect close printed at a single exact price. Two traders are now long the move that followed, and to any eye but the trained one they are in the same trade, side by side, equally right. They are not equal, and they were never in the same trade. This reading walks the closing gates of the Sequence, the frame with its measurement, the signature that fills it, and the invalidation, and it shows what the book has shown from the first page, that precision is the line between traders, and that the line does not disappear at the moment of execution. It runs straight through it.

RECALL THE GROUND. A campaign advancing, a re-accumulation completed within it, a sidelong structure that purged its own low and bought it straight back. That low, swept and refused, is the authoring structure, and just above it sits a single price, the exact location where the reclaim signed. Both traders saw the reclaim. Both are long. Their open profit will move together for the next few minutes, and a stranger watching both screens would swear they held the same position. The stranger is the untrained eye, and he is about to be taught the difference between a price and a neighborhood.

The first trader never had the price, so he did what the imprecise always do. He drew a zone. A band around the reclaim a few points deep, wide enough that price could not fail to be inside it somewhere, and he worked the band as if it were a location. He put on a first position high in it, where he judged the turn might already have come, and when price traded lower he added a second nearer the swept low, and he called this scaling in and a better average. Two entries, an averaged fill, a position smeared across a band. What he never had, and could not have, was the one thing a band cannot hold: the exact price, and with it the signature, the perfect close that prints at that price and at no other. You cannot collect a signature you were not present for, and he was never at the price. He was long, he was early, he was approximate, and on the screen he looked precisely like a man in a good trade.

The second trader had marked the single price and he waited for it, and he did nothing at all until it came. He let the perfect close print at the exact location, the signature, and he executed on it, one order, one fill, the price the entire idea turns upon. Everything the frame then asked of him could be answered honestly, because the answers were measured from a true point. The death line went beneath the authoring low, a real and surveyed distance away. The size fell out as the quotient of that distance and nothing else. The target was projected to where independent witnesses converged. Precision at the entry made every later number precise. Had he entered a band instead, each of those numbers would have inherited the band's vagueness: a death line measured from an average that meant nothing, a size computed from a distance that was never real. He wrote the frame where it could not be unwritten, and surrendered the right to move any of it.

Then the market breathed, as it nearly always does before it pays. Price slipped back off the reclaim, down through the first trader's higher entry, already a loss, and into the band he had averaged across. His line, if he had drawn one, sat somewhere in that band at a price he could not quite defend, and the ordinary hostility of the move either took it or left him clutching a poor average with an unclear grave beneath it. The same breath ran down to the second trader's exact entry, touched the price the market had to reach and refuse, and stopped above the death line beneath the authoring low, which was never in danger because it had been placed outside the measured envelope. It held. The low held with it, the buyers returned, and the leg turned up toward the target the witnesses had named. Both men were still, in some loose sense, in the trade. Only one of them was in it on terms he could survive.

Set them side by side and the difference is the same difference the book has named at every truth. It is not courage, or patience, or the idea, which was one idea. It is precision. The zone is the shape imprecision takes when it needs to look like a decision. Two entries in a band is not a method, it is a confession that the location was never found, dressed as prudence. And the signature, the single close that separates a real location from a hopeful one, cannot be collected in a band at all, because it happens at a price, and the man spread across a neighborhood was never standing at that price to be paid. The untrained eye sees two longs and calls them one trade. The trained eye sees one exact and one approximate, and knows by now what the whole book has repeated, that approximate is not a gentler kind of right. It is only a slower road to wrong.

Name the closing gates this reading walked, and notice that only one trader truly walked them. The frame, honest only because an exact entry made its numbers real. The signature, which the precise trader alone could hold, printed at the price he had the discipline to wait for. And the invalidation, set beneath the true structure because the entry itself was true, then surrendered to. One trader stands on the exact price with a clean line beneath him. The other stands in a zone with a smeared average and a grave he cannot locate, calls it the same trade, and will blame the market when it proves not to be. What the precise trader now does as his position runs, the harvest taken in pieces and the grave that must never creep up toward the profit, is the work of the last reading.

PART IV

CONTINUITY

CHAPTER 10

REPETITION

The Gait

The market never repeats its moves exactly, but never stops reflecting them. The next pullback borrows the character of the last; the coming leg is measured in the image of the one before; the journey underway inherits the habits of the campaign that authored it. Do not memorize the market's shape. Learn its gait. Shapes change with every session. The gait holds while the campaign holds, and when the gait breaks, the market has changed its mind about something, and so must you.

TRANSGRESSION OF THE TRUTH

ON THE EVENING OF the eighteenth of August, 1913, at the casino of Monte Carlo, a roulette wheel began the most famous streak in the history of probability. Black came up. Then black again. Then again. By the time the run reached ten, word had traveled through the gaming rooms and a crowd was pressing around the table; by fifteen, the table was buried in money, and nearly all of it was on red. The reasoning was unanimous and felt unanswerable: the wheel had produced a monstrosity, the law of averages was being violated before their eyes, and every additional black deepened the debt that red was now owed. Men doubled and redoubled, staking fortunes on the certainty that the universe must shortly balance its books. Black came up the sixteenth time, and the seventeenth, and the twentieth, and the crowd, far from retreating, escalated, because each impossible black made red more inevitable still. The wheel ran black twenty-six times in succession. The house won millions of francs in a few hours, and it won them, note carefully, without any edge beyond the zero mattering: the players were not beaten by the odds. They were beaten by their own reading of the past.

Perform the autopsy, because these gamblers were not fools ignoring history; they were students of history who had learned the wrong lesson from it. They watched the record with total attention, computed from it, and staked everything on their computation. Their error was one this book can now name with precision: they read repetition as obligation. To them, the streak was a debt accumulating, each black a further borrowing against a red that must eventually be repaid, as though the wheel kept books and honored them. But a roulette wheel is the one machine on earth engineered to remember nothing. Each spin is an orphan: no memory, no campaign, no crowd persisting from one turn to the next, and therefore no habit and no debt. The past of a memoryless machine constrains nothing at all, and twenty-six blacks made the twenty-seventh spin precisely as even as the first. The players stood before a process with no character, and read character into it, and paid what readers of phantom character always pay.

Now mark the double edge, because the market is not a roulette wheel, and that is exactly what makes this transgression dangerous rather than merely stupid. The market does carry memory: positions persist, campaigns persist, the crowd that drove yesterday's leg is substantially the crowd defending it today. Repetition in markets is therefore genuinely informative, and this chapter is about harvesting it. But the gambler's fallacy survives the transfer intact, wearing better clothes. It has climbed six days running, it is due a red one. This pullback has run further than the last three, it must snap back. The trader who reasons this way has imported the Monte Carlo error into an arena where it is harder to see, because here the past really does speak. The distinction the whole chapter turns upon is this: the market's past constrains the character of what follows. It never, under any circumstance, creates a debt. Due is should wearing a statistician's coat, and the second truth's ban applies to it in full.

INTERPRETATION

THE TRANSGRESSION GENERALIZES INTO the two ways of misreading any streak, and every trader alive leans toward one of them. The continuation error assumes the pattern must persist: six green days become a regime that cannot end, and the trader buys the seventh at the top of the governing range, paying double premium for a habit at its most advertised. The reversion error assumes the pattern must stop: the same six days become an overextension that owes the world a collapse, and the trader sells into a campaign whose character has shown no crack whatever, standing in front of the removal van the fourth truth warned about. Both errors share one root: they convert observation into obligation, description into debt. The fluent reading does neither. It says: this is how the market has been behaving, that behavior will tend to persist while its authors persist, and my expectation of its persistence is a frame condition, to be confirmed rung by rung, never an entitlement. The past is a witness, and an excellent one. It is never a guarantor.

OBSERVANCE OF THE TRUTH

IN 1857 A YOUNG Mississippi steersman named Samuel Clemens, not yet calling himself Mark Twain, apprenticed himself to a pilot named Horace Bixby, and was handed the most impossible curriculum in American professional life. A pilot, Bixby informed him, must know the river: twelve hundred miles of it, every point, bar, bend, crossing, and snag, by name, in order, upstream and downstream, by day and in pitch darkness. The boy set to memorizing with a notebook and despair, and just as the shape of the river began to settle into his head, he made the discovery that broke his heart: the river would not stay. Banks caved in the night. Bars built and dissolved with the seasons. Channels wandered; landmarks drowned; the river he had memorized last month had partly ceased to exist by this one. He put the objection to Bixby in something like anguish: what is the use of learning a thing that will not hold still? And Bixby's answer is the observance of this truth entire: you learn the river's shape with absolute certainty, and then you steer by the shape in your head, reading the water for what has changed, because the shape changes but the river's ways do not.

What the cub eventually acquired was not a map but a fluency, and Twain's account of it in Life on the Mississippi remains the finest description of professional reading ever set down. The face of the water became a book, he wrote, a dead language to the passenger but one that told the pilot its mind. A faint dimple on the surface, and the pilot knew a deadly snag lay beneath; a certain slant of ripple announced a bluff reef where the boat would strike, while an almost identical ripple meant a wind reef, mere breeze on water, that a captain could steam through untroubled. The marks looked the same. The habits behind them differed, and the pilot distinguished killer from illusion not by the shape of the mark but by its behavior in context: where it lay against the bend, how it held as the light changed, what the river had been doing upstream. Nothing on that surface repeated exactly, ever. Everything on it reflected: the same causes writing the same signatures in endlessly varied hands, legible to the man who had learned the handwriting rather than memorizing any single page.

And there was a further layer, the one that made piloting a profession rather than a knack: the river's changes themselves had character. A rising river behaved one way, hunting through the low ground and opening chutes that a falling river would close and turn fatal; a caving bank foretold its collapse in stages a pilot learned to expect; the shifting of a bar followed the habits of current and season. The pilot did not merely tolerate the river's changes; he anticipated them, because change itself repeated its manners. This is why Bixby's men could run a black, starless reach at full steam with the shape of last month's river in their heads and this night's water on their faces: they held the reflection, not the replica, and they corrected the picture by the gait of the thing, mile by mile. The passengers below saw recklessness. What was actually aboard was the most disciplined act of reading in America, performed on a text that rewrote itself daily and never once changed its style.

INTERPRETATION

THE PILOT IS THE trader this entire chapter is trying to build. He does not predict the river; he recognizes it. His knowledge is not a photograph but a grammar of habits: what a snag's dimple does, how a rising river hunts, the manner in which a bank confesses before it caves. When the water shows him something, he asks the reader's question, what is this behaving like, and never the tourist's question, what does this look like. Traders, overwhelmingly, are tourists: they memorize the shapes of past charts, the photographs of patterns, and they drown at the first bend that wears a familiar face over an unfamiliar bottom, because a shape carried out of its context is exactly as treacherous on a chart as on the river. The sixth truth taught that patterns are words. This truth adds the deeper unit: beneath the words, the market has a voice, a characteristic way of moving that persists across its endlessly novel sentences, and fluency at this level, the level of manner rather than shape, is what separates the pilot from the passenger holding the same map.

KEYS TO THE TRUTH

STATE THE DOCTRINE PLAINLY, because it is the working heart of the chapter. The market does not replicate its prior moves. It reflects them closely. And the reflection runs deeper than geometry. The eighth truth already harvested the geometric layer: the measured move, the swing projection, the completed leg casting the length of the next. What almost no one harvests is the stylistic layer. The character of the prior structure is the best available forecast of the character of the next. Watch the pullbacks inside a delivering campaign. They are the market's signature written small. Suppose the campaign has corrected shallow, quick, and calm. Then the anticipation is that the next correction arrives shallow, quick, and calm. It is an anticipation you may frame. A campaign that corrects deep and sharp advertises that its next correction will bite the same way. Trade the reflection of the past. At the very least, let it tell you where to become involved. The shallow-pullback campaign will not reach the generous discount you are waiting for. The deep-pullback campaign will punish the trader who boards at the first polite dip. The style of the journey already told you the price of the ticket.

Give the intuition its proper name: the gait. You know your oldest friend at three hundred meters, in poor light, in a crowd. Not by his face, which distance erased, but by his walk, which nothing erases. A gait belongs to the body, not to the wardrobe. Market campaigns have gaits. One trend strides: long efficient legs, brief regular rests, corrections that barely trouble the prior swing. Another trudges: laboring advances, deep exhausted retracements, progress bought at overlap. The two may be drawing identical shapes on a chart of identical slope. They are as different as two men. The difference is the tradeable information. The gait tells you how this campaign takes its steps, and therefore how to time yours. It tells you where it will pause and how hard it will pull back. It shows you what its resting looks like as opposed to its dying. Identify the campaign by its gait before you trade its shape. Shapes are worn like coats, and the market owns a thousand. The gait is the body underneath.

Why should character persist at all? The answer is the fifth truth's kind of answer: mechanical, and mercifully free of mystique. A campaign is one crowd doing one thing. The participants who drove the leg are substantially the participants defending it. The hands absorbing each dip this week are the hands that absorbed them last week. They operate at the same scale, with the same urgency, under the same instructions. Habits of movement are the visible signature of that crowd's composition and intent. Patient size absorbs quietly and produces the shallow, calm correction. Nervous leverage produces the deep, violent one. While the crowd persists, the campaign's manners persist, and that is why the reflection is trustworthy. And the converse is the chapter's most valuable sentence. When the manners change, the crowd has changed. When the crowd has changed, the campaign you mapped may no longer exist. Character does not break for no reason. It breaks because the authorship changed hands.

Your concession that this reading carries a subjective element was honest. The discipline of this book can shrink that element to a residue. Character is measurable as a trio. Every instrument in the trio you already own. Depth: each correction as a fraction of the leg it corrects, a number. Duration: each correction in parcels of time, the fifth truth's coin, a number. Delivery: efficient or labored, the sixth truth's binary verdict. Record the trio for the corrections the campaign has already printed. The character then stops being an impression and becomes an envelope. This campaign corrects a third of its legs, in a session or less, without labor. Now the anticipation is a frame condition in the second truth's grammar. The next correction has held the envelope, or it has not. Two observers agree. What remains subjective is only the synthesis, the pilot's feel for the whole water. And that is where subjectivity belongs. It sits at the top of a stack of objective measurements, never at the bottom holding everything up.

Now the doctrine's finest edge: the character-break as diagnostic. Consider the correction that violates the recorded envelope. The deep gouge in a campaign of shallow dips. The three-session sprawl in a market that had rested by the hour. It has not merely inconvenienced your entry. It has impeached your map. Something you believed about this journey, its location, its destination, the campaign behind it, is now in doubt. The crowd whose habits you measured is no longer behaving like itself. Crowds do not change their manners while their circumstances stand still. This is the earliest warning system the market offers, and it fires before the levels do. Structure breaks at the end of a campaign's failure, but character breaks first. The gait falters while the shape still holds. The third truth taught you to hear the train braking in open country. This is the finer ear. The train is still running, on time, but running differently. The seasoned commuter is already gathering his coat.

The application to engagement is direct, and it feeds both of the truths behind you. Involvement is timed to the recorded character. In the shallow-quick campaign, you position within the modest envelope its habits offer. You enter at the re-accumulation the reflection nominates. You do not wait for a discount its manners have never once granted. In the deep-sharp campaign, you wait, unbothered, through the first polite dip that tempts the impatient. The recorded character promises the real invitation runs deeper. And the ninth truth's grave inherits the same information. The death line and the character envelope should agree. A correction that exceeds both the structural grave and the recorded manner has said the same thing twice. Where character bounds and structure bounds coincide, your invalidation is not one measurement but two witnesses concurring. You know from the fifth truth what concurring witnesses make: a preponderance.

The reflection reads at every scale the fifth truth's telescope offers. The day trader's version deserves its own sentence, because sessions reflect sessions. Yesterday's character is the single best sketch of today available before today begins. How did the day open relative to its value? Did the early range hold or break? Did the session trend in one campaign or rotate home? Days, like campaigns, are authored by crowds. The crowd that assembles at tomorrow's open is substantially the crowd that went home at tonight's close. It carries the same positions, the same intentions, and the same unfinished business. A market that has spent three sessions rotating inside a range is showing you rotation's gait. The fourth open is presumed guilty of the same conduct until the character breaks. A market that has trended on schedule for a week owes you nothing. But it has told you what its mornings look like when the campaign is working. Read yesterday the way the pilot read the last mile of water. It is not a promise of the next mile. It is the best available draft of it.

For the purest specimen of reflection read honestly, take the man who found the solar system's gait. Johannes Kepler inherited, in Tycho Brahe's observations, the finest record of planetary behavior ever compiled. He inherited with it two thousand years of instruction about what the record must show. Circles, the perfect motion of the heavens, sanctified from Aristotle to Copernicus. For years Kepler tried to fit Mars to a circle. The fit failed, by eight minutes of arc. That is a sliver smaller than anything the naked eye resolves. Every predecessor would have shrugged the error into the instruments. Kepler refused the shrug, on the grounds that

Tycho's record was better than that. He let eight minutes of arc overrule twenty centuries of authority. The orbit was an ellipse. The heavens had a gait of their own, and it was not the one the books demanded. The man who read the reflection in the data rather than the doctrine in his head walked out of the library holding the actual laws of planetary motion. Every trader inherits his own two thousand years. The patterns he was taught must appear. The cycles the course promised. Kepler's discipline is the chapter's: when the record and the doctrine disagree by even eight minutes, the record is telling you the truth.

Put the whole doctrine on the screen once, in the pilot's chair. A campaign is delivering. You hold the map from the third truth and the appraisal from the fourth. The record shows two corrections so far: a third of the leg, a session or less, no labor in the give-back. Textbook rest inside a striding gait. The third correction begins. Now you are not watching price. You are watching manner. It reaches a third of the leg and slows: the envelope holding. It finds the region your reflection nominated for re-accumulation, at an hour the fifth truth approves. The sixth truth's verdicts begin to print: the probe below the shallow swing, taken and refused inside the parcel. Everything the campaign has ever done, it is doing again. You engage, with the ninth truth's grave set beneath an accumulation that two witnesses, structure and character, agree upon. Or the other morning arrives. The correction knifes through a third, then through a half, laboring nowhere, resting nowhere. Your instruments all say the same quiet thing: this is not how this campaign behaves. You do not need a level to break to act on that sentence. The gait has broken. The authorship is in question. The map goes back on the table before the structure has conceded a thing. That is trading the reflection, and its other name is piloting.

One boundary stone, before the Image, to keep this truth honest in your hands: a reflection requires something to reflect. Three recorded corrections make a character worth framing. One makes an anecdote. An anecdote projected forward is just the gambler's ghost returning with better vocabulary. The envelope tightens as the campaign lengthens. Your reliance should scale with the record. Early in a campaign, character is a hypothesis held loosely. Deep in one, it is among the most trustworthy instruments you own. And remember at every scale what the fifth truth taught about the telescope. Campaigns nest inside campaigns. Each has its own gait, the governing stride and the local step, reflected at every magnification. Read the gait of the frame you trade, inside the gait of the frame that governs it. The two together will tell you most of what the day is willing to disclose in advance.

IMAGE

The Gait. You know your oldest friend at three hundred meters, at dusk, across a crowded square: not his face, which the distance has taken, but his walk, which nothing takes. He may change his coat, his city, his fortunes, and you will know him from the bridge before he clears the corner, because the gait belongs to the body itself. And should he one evening walk differently, shorter in the stride, favoring a side, you will know before any doctor and almost before he does that something has happened to him. The market wears a thousand faces and cannot disguise its walk. Learn gaits, not faces, and notice the limp the moment it begins.

AUTHORITY

"The face of the water, in time, became a wonderful book—a book that was a dead language to the uneducated passenger, but which told me its mind without reserve, delivering its most cherished secrets as clearly as if it uttered them with a voice. And it was not a book to be read once and thrown aside, for it had a new story to tell every day." — Mark Twain, Life on the Mississippi, 1883

REVERSAL

THE FIRST CORRUPTION IS the market's own doing, and it is aimed at you personally: the habit everyone can see stops paying. A character legible only to the careful is an edge; a character advertised widely enough becomes bait, because the market's most sophisticated participants harvest the expectations of the rest. The pullback that has held the same depth four times running is, by the fifth, an expectation with money leaning on it, and expectations with money leaning on them are exactly what sweeps are made from. This does not repeal the chapter; reflection remains the best forecast of manner that exists. It stipulates humility about freshness: the reflection is most trustworthy when least famous, and a habit that has become the crowd's open secret should be traded in the knowledge that its next repetition is the one most likely to be mined. The gait is the body, yes. But bodies that are watched learn to feint.

The second corruption you have already met at the roulette table, and it will re-enter your trading wearing this chapter as a disguise: reflection hardened into obligation. The campaign has corrected shallow five times, and somewhere in the sixth wait the trader stops framing the anticipation and starts collecting the debt: the market owes him a shallow pullback, and when the correction runs deeper he adds instead of re-examining, Monte Carlo logic on a chart, doubling on red because black has gone on too long. The character envelope is a frame condition, confirmable and refutable like everything else in your process; the moment it becomes an entitlement, you have stopped reading the market's habits and started billing the market for them, and the market pays no invoices. Anticipate the reflection. Position for it, frame it, measure it. And hold it exactly as loosely as the pilot holds last month's river: steering by the shape in his head, eyes open on tonight's water, ready in every mile for the bank that caved this afternoon.

You now hold the market's habits in one hand and, from the truths before, the death of any single claim in the other, and the tension between them points at what remains. Habits are read across many trades; verdicts arrive one trade at a time; and no quantity of fluent reading converts into an equity curve without the machinery that carries you from each trade to the series, indifferent to any single outcome. The pilot ran the river nightly for years, and it was the running, not any single reach, that made the profession. The eleventh truth is that machinery: Process.

CHAPTER 11

PROCESS

The Toll Road

You are not paid to be right. You are paid to operate a machine that harvests the market's journeys: a machine that files claims, buries the dead ones, collects at every station, and runs identically on its best day and its worst. Right and wrong are the vocabulary of spectators. Protect the account, pay the account along the way, and let the market keep the score it was always going to keep. The trade is an event. The process is the business.

TRANSGRESSION OF THE TRUTH

NO ONE HAS EVER read markets better than Jesse Livermore, and the claim is barely contested even now. He began at fourteen, posting quotations on a broker's board in Boston, and discovered that the numbers spoke to him: he could feel the tape gathering itself before a move the way sailors feel weather. The bucket shops of New England banned him one by one for winning. In the panic of 1907 he was reported to have taken a million dollars from the short side in a single day, and the legend runs that the great Morgan himself sent word asking him to stop selling. In the autumn of 1929 he assembled one of the most celebrated positions in the history of speculation, short the entire boiling market, and when the crash came the newspapers needed someone to blame and chose him. His fortune that year was reported in figures that made him one of the richest men in America. He possessed, decades before this book gave them names, nearly every truth in it: he read the language, respected location, waited on time, probed before he committed. As pure perception, the man was the summit. That is precisely what makes his ledger the most frightening document in trading.

Because he told us the rules himself. The book built from his life, and the memoir he later wrote in his own name, amount to a catalogue of process this chapter could have copied out: never average a losing position; sell down to the sleeping point; the big money is made in the waiting, not the trading; probe with small size and add only as the market proves the idea. He knew all of it, wrote all of it, said all of it aloud. And he was ruined four times. The ruins were not mysteries; he audited them himself with the same clear eye he turned on the tape, and each audit returned the same finding: he had broken his own rules. The cotton affair of 1908 is the type specimen. A persuasive expert named Percy Thomas talked with him for hours, and the greatest tape reader alive stopped reading the tape and started believing a man; he bought cotton against his own system, and when it went against him he averaged down, the one act he had forbidden above all others, and he fed the position until a fortune of millions was gone. He did not lack the rule. The rule was his. He lacked whatever it is that makes a rule stronger than an evening's conversation.

Name what that missing thing was, because his whole calamity turns on it: nothing outside his own skull enforced anything. No frame owned him once a trial opened; no fuse existed that he could not unscrew with a phone call; no separation of powers stood between the man who took positions and the man who judged them. His discipline and his impulses were roommates, and under pressure the impulses held the lease. This book opened with a general who was his own method and died of it, and Livermore is the same architecture in a different uniform: when he was fresh and the theater suited him, the gift performed miracles, and each recovery persuaded him again that the gift was the whole requirement. The machine was him. And him wore out, as every him does. He went through bankruptcy in 1915 and rebuilt; he was broken again in the thirties and this time the rebuilding failed; in 1940 he published a careful little book laying out, one more time, the rules he had never been able to obey, and in November of that year he died by his own hand, leaving a note that said his life had been a failure. The market's greatest reader was never once defeated by his reading. He was defeated, four times and finally, by the absence of a machine to keep what the reading won.

INTERPRETATION

LIVERMORE CLOSES AN ARGUMENT that every trader eventually has with himself: the belief that sufficient knowledge will substitute for process. Here was more knowledge of markets than any of us will accumulate, joined to rules he had personally written in his own blood, and it did not hold, because rules that live in the head are weather. They blow away under exactly the pressure they were written for, and the seventh truth told you why: every decision is made twice, and the second decision-maker, the one in the fire, does not read memoirs. If the finest perception in the history of the business could not keep its winnings without external machinery, then the question is settled for everyone below that summit, which is everyone.

And mark the crueler mechanism: his fortunes were the trap. Each recovery, each mountain rebuilt by pure gift, taught him at the deepest level that the gift sufficed, that process was for lesser readers. Winning without process is the most expensive education in trading precisely because it feels like the cheapest: it certifies the absence of the one thing that would have made the winning permanent. Observe the asymmetry his life proves: his reading compounded for forty years, growing sharper to the end; his account did not compound at all, arriving where it started and then below it. Reading is a skill, and skills accrue to the person. Keeping is a system, and systems must be built outside the person, or the person will spend them.

OBSERVANCE OF THE TRUTH

WALK THE FLOOR OF any casino on earth and you are inside the counterargument, built in marble and staffed around the clock. The house has no opinion about the next card, the next spin, the next roll. It cannot tell you what the wheel will do, and it has never needed to know. What it has instead is a small measured edge and an enormous machine for harvesting it. Look at the machine's parts with this book's eyes. Table limits: no single bet, however rich the guest, may ever threaten the enterprise; size is capped by policy, not by the pit boss's nerve. Payout rules: fixed, printed, agreed before any wager, the frame that owns the house once play begins. Procedures: the shuffle, the deal, the settlement, identical at every table, every hour, the sequence drilled past reflex into furniture. Surveillance and the count: the record, kept by parties who did not make the decisions, audited nightly. The most profitable trading operation most people will ever stand inside contains not one forecast, and every component of it is a chapter of this book wearing a uniform.

Now watch the single most instructive motion on the floor: the croupier's rake. Hand after hand, the house's percentage is swept off the felt and dropped through a slot into a locked box beneath the table. The house does not let its winnings ride. It does not leave its profit on the table to see how big the night can get; it collects continuously, at every station of every hand of every shift, converting variance into salary while the game is still being played. The drop box is the casino's confession of this chapter's doctrine: the most successful gambling operation in history is history's most relentless taker of partial profits. And notice, too, the payoff of a seed planted ten chapters ago: the house is boring on purpose. Identical rooms, identical procedures, identical hours; thrill is the product it sells, never the product it consumes. Excitement is for the customers. The customers, on the whole, pay for it.

And study the house on its losing nights, because it has them constantly and reveals its soul in how it takes them. A whale runs hot and the table bleeds millions, and the house pays out smiling, comps the suite, and changes nothing: no revenge, no doubled limits, no manager overruling the payout rules to win it back tonight. Tomorrow the same tables open at the same limits under the same procedures, because the house's confidence has never lived at the level of the night. It lives at the level of the series, where a small edge multiplied by an uncountable number of hands is not a hope but an arithmetic destiny. The casino has losing nights and no losing years. That sentence is the entire psychology of process, and no one in the building had to be brave to achieve it. The machine carries the conviction, so the staff can carry trays.

INTERPRETATION

PUT THE TWO ESTABLISHMENTS side by side, the greatest reader and the reading-free machine, and let the contrast close the case. Livermore was right about markets more often and more brilliantly than perhaps anyone who has lived, and he kept, at the end, nothing. The house is right about nothing, forecasts nothing, perceives nothing, and keeps its percentage of everything, decade upon decade, through wars and depressions and every regime the markets can turn. If being right were the business, the results would run the other way. They do not, because the business is what this chapter says it is: the operation of a harvesting machine, and the machine outperforms the genius over any series long enough to matter. The retail trader spends his years trying to become Livermore. The professional spends them building a personal casino: limits, procedures, a rake, a count.

See also what the machine does for the operator's inner life, because it is the bridge to everything this chapter has been building toward. Nobody who works in a casino tilts about a spin, and not because casinos hire saints: the payout table cannot be edited by an employee's feelings, and so the feelings, having no lever to pull, retire. Your frames are your payout table; your process is your procedure manual; the ninth truth already separated your powers. What remains is to install the rake, the continuous self-payment that makes the whole enterprise durable, and that is where your doctrine now enters.

KEYS TO THE TRUTH

BEGIN BY PROSECUTING THE culture. It is the true transgressor behind the man. Trading talk runs on a binary: right or wrong, win or lose. Its harvest rules follow the same binary. The full target is glory. The partial is acceptable. And the partial that precedes a full run earns the most corrosive sentence in the language: should have held. Examine that sentence with a lawyer's eye. It collapses. It convicts a decision using evidence from the future, information that did not exist at the moment of the act. That is hindsight accounting. No discipline on earth audits its operators that way. The pilot who diverted around the storm that later dissipated is not written up for cowardice. The surgeon who ordered the test that came back clean is not billed for waste. Process domains judge decisions by the information available and the procedure followed. Trading, done properly, has only two honest verdicts, and neither of them is right or wrong: process followed, process breached. The first truth ruled that a breach is an error whatever the outcome. The ninth added that obedience is never an error whatever the outcome. This chapter completes the triad. The outcome was never yours to be judged by at all. It belongs to the market. The market was always going to keep its own score.

Then fix the objective, in plain words. The culture has that backwards too. The objective is not to be right. It is not to require perfection of the market. It is to protect the account, and to add to the account along the train's route to its destination. Hold both halves. The account is not the scoreboard. It is the instrument. It is the one machine part that cannot be replaced. Protecting it means protecting the ability to run the process tomorrow. Every arithmetic in this book, the quotient, the series, the expectancy, silently assumes there is a next trade. A trader can survive years of modest reading if the account survives with him. He cannot survive one season of brilliance that leaves no account to be brilliant with. Livermore is buried in that sentence.

See also what the full-target culture is actually demanding. Named plainly, it embarrasses itself: it requires perfection of the market. The terminal-to-terminal trade is held through everything. It pays only when the market travels the entire surveyed route without any renegotiation deep enough to reach a stop or unseat a nervous holder. The tenth truth told you how markets actually travel: in legs and reflections, advancing and renegotiating. The journey is interrupted at every station by the auction doing its ordinary work. A process that profits only when the market behaves perfectly is a process built to lose to the market's routine behavior. The harvest doctrine asks the market for nothing unusual. Reach the next station, as journeys almost always do, and the toll is paid. Requiring less of the market is how you receive more from it. The full-TP purist demands everything. He is structurally positioned to keep receiving nothing.

Now the harvest doctrine, the machinery of paying yourself. Every component of it was built in the chapters behind you. The journey to a destination passes sub-locations: the intermediate stations of the third truth. There the tenth truth taught you a reflection pullback is due. The market renegotiates at the places where business was done. At those stations, the process collects. Take some off, or all, as your frame prescribed in the cool hour. Let the correction you had every reason to expect run its course without you aboard. Then wait for the re-accumulation to complete and the sixth truth's signature to print. When the objective markers and the hour align again, re-enter in the same direction, on a fresh claim, at the discount the correction built. Run the arithmetic of that round trip. Notice what the full-TP culture never computes. You exited at a premium and re-entered at value. You harvested the swing and improved your basis. The campaign is still yours. Done at the stations the frame named, partial profit is not caution. It is offense: the same journey ridden twice, paid twice, at better prices than the man who white-knuckled through the pullback he was warned about by his own map.

And the rake has a mirror. The phrase to hold is protect and add. The machine does both with the same motion. The capital collected at one station is the capital the frame's addition clause deploys at the next re-accumulation. Harvested at premium, redeployed at discount, the campaign ridden in waves rather than in one white-knuckled hold. This is what the seventh truth's pre-authorized addition was always for. Not averaging into pain, but compounding into confirmation. Each wave is funded by the last one's toll. Each add stands on a fresh signature with its own grave. The full-TP trader and the wave rider can finish the same campaign with the same final chart. The wave rider has taken more out of it with less ever at risk. He treated the journey as the market treats it: as a series of negotiations, each one payable.

Beneath the arithmetic sits a deeper purpose. It deserves to be said without decoration. The harvested capital is armored against the day you are simply wrong. That day is not a risk. It is a schedule. The tenth truth taught that maps get impeached, that character breaks, that the best-read campaign can be re-authored overnight. Every truth in this book assumes a fallible reader. That is the only kind there is. Paying yourself along the way is the premium on that certainty. Eventually the market produces the surprise that no sequence could have caught. When it does, it matters enormously whether it surprises a paid man or a hopeful one. The paid man reads the impeachment with interest and re-surveys. The hopeful man, everything still riding, reads it with dread and denial. And dread and denial are how surprises become disasters. The rake is not about greed or fear. It is about which man you are when the inevitable arrives.

Sometimes the re-accumulation never completes. The pullback deepens into a character break. The campaign dies with your harvest banked and your remaining piece stopped at its structural grave. Understand what happened, because the culture will read it upside down. The culture calls it luck: got out just in time. The process calls it design functioning. The toll was collected before the bridge washed out, exactly as the tollkeeper's architecture intended. The partial turns out to have been the only profit that journey ever truly offered. No one at the casino calls the drop box lucky. The re-entry that never came was not a missed trade. It was the else-nothing verdict doing its work on a claim the market declined to re-validate. The full-TP trader on the same journey donated his open profit back at the impeachment. He calls your result fortune. Let him. His accounting convicts pilots for diverting.

Zoom out to the level where all of this becomes livable, the level the house never leaves: the series. The eighth truth gave every trade one meter, the unit. A hundred trades could then be read as one experiment. Here is the psychological dividend of that arithmetic. Outcome-indifference at the scale of the episode is impossible for anyone whose episode is his verdict. It is easy for anyone whose verdict lives at the scale of the series. Nobody can shrug at a coin flip that decides his worth. Anyone can shrug at one hand of ten thousand whose edge he has measured. The trader who suffers over individual trades is not weak. He is mis-scaled. He carries at the level of the event a judgment that only exists at the level of the ledger. Process is, among everything else, the relocation of your identity from the trade to the series. The series is the only address where the truth about you is kept.

Run the arithmetic of the two architectures across a year. The compounding decides the argument. The terminal bettor's results arrive in rare large chunks, separated by droughts and full retraces. His equity curve is hostage to whether a handful of journeys complete perfectly. The toll collector's results arrive continuously, in smaller certain pieces plus the occasional completed runner. Every collected toll is capital that compounds from that day instead of remaining hostage on the table. Variance is not just discomfort. It is cost. Capital exposed is capital that cannot yet be resized, redeployed, or compounded. The house understood this before any of us was born. The drop box does not merely protect the night's revenue. It puts the revenue to work in tomorrow's float while the terminal bettors are still waiting to find out if they were ever paid at all.

The machine requires maintenance. The maintenance is itself a scheduled part of the machine, not a mood that follows bad weeks. The ninth truth's autopsy generalizes into the standing audit. On a fixed cadence, weekly or by block of trades, the ledger is read with the only questions that improve anything. Which losses were tuition, and which were leakage? Which steps of the sequence were breached, at which hour, in which state? Which frames validated and were not filed, and why? Where was the harvest taken at stations, and where was it fear wearing the rake's uniform? The audit's output is levers: specific, controllable adjustments to a specific step. That is all improvement has ever been made of. The house counts the drop every night. Not because it distrusts the arithmetic, but because a machine uncounted is a machine already drifting. Count your drop.

If you want to feel the destination of all this, read a week of it written down. The texture is the proof. Monday: two claims framed, one validated at the station on signature, first toll collected at sub-location as filed, runner stopped behind the advancing structure. Process followed, plus one unit and change. Tuesday: no claims validated. The else-nothing verdict twice. Flat. Wednesday: entered on signature, premise impeached by character break before the stop, buried at premise-death per the frame. Process followed, minus half a unit. Thursday: framed harvest at the second station, re-entry claim filed but never validated. Process followed, plus one unit. Friday: breach logged, one entry taken a step early in the sequence, tagged leakage, lever identified, size unaffected. Minus a quarter unit, and the only real loss of the week. Read it back. It is a shift report, and it is supposed to be. Somewhere in a week like that, the culture would be shouting about the trade that ran three stations past your last toll. The report does not record that event. It happened in a jurisdiction you no longer live in.

IMAGE

The Toll Road. The road knows nothing of destinations. It neither asks where a traveler is bound nor cares whether he arrives; it collects at every gate, a fixed toll at a fixed barrier, journey after journey, in rain and in boom. The keeper never wagers the road's revenue on any traveler completing his trip, for travelers are variance and gates are income, and the road outlasts every carriage that ever rolled it. Build your trading as the road is built: gates at the stations your map has surveyed, collection at each gate as a matter of architecture, and no opinion whatsoever about where anyone is finally going.

AUTHORITY

"I owe my fortune to never buying at the bottom, and always selling too soon." — attributed to Nathan Mayer Rothschild

REVERSAL

PROCESS FOSSILIZES, AND THE fossil looks exactly like discipline until the market has fully moved on. The machine that cannot change is only the mirror image of the trader who cannot commit: both have stopped listening. Markets migrate, characters turn over, the stations that paid for a year go quiet, and the process that meets this with pure obedience becomes a toll road on an abandoned route, immaculately operated, collecting nothing. The answer is not flexibility in the fire, which is just breach wearing a robe; it is the amendment clause your audit already contains. The process is changed the way constitutions are changed: deliberately, in the cool hour, on the evidence of the series, never on the pain of an episode. A rule revised after thirty trades of counted evidence is evolution. A rule revised on a bad Tuesday is Livermore listening to Percy Thomas, and it has the same sequel.

And the rake corrupts, in the one direction this chapter has made attractive: partials decay into fear. The trader discovers the drop box and begins sweeping the felt at the first tick of green, everywhere, at no station in particular, harvesting not where the map named gates but wherever his pulse rose; his winners are amputated at the ankle while his losers still run to their full graves, and he calls the wreckage prudence because it resembles the doctrine. Hold the line where it was always drawn: the harvest points are framed, in advance, at the sub-locations the survey nominated, exactly as the entry and the death line were. A toll collected at a gate is architecture. A toll collected in open country because the keeper got nervous is not collection at all; it is flight with a cash box. If the partial was not in the frame, it was not process. It was the fire, deciding again.

There remains one more thing the machine produces, and it is the most valuable output on the whole floor, though it never appears in the count. Run the process long enough, legibly enough, and it begins to build something in the operator: a quietness that the industry spends fortunes trying to sell separately, bottled as mindset, as discipline, as psychology. It cannot be bottled. It can only be grown, and what grows it is everything this book has built, in the order it was built. Why the person is the last thing to be assembled, and why the industry has the assembly exactly backwards, is the final truth: Psychology.

A FOURTH READING

THE LEG THAT STOPPED BEHAVING LIKE ITSELF

This reading adds no gate to the Sequence. It shows what the gates were for once the entry is already right: the harvest taken in pieces, the invalidation left unmoved, and the character watched for the moment a winner stops behaving like one.

THE EARLIER READINGS WATCHED a market located, framed, and tried. This one watches what happens after all of that is done right and the trade is already a winner, because that is where most of the money ever made is quietly given back. The scene is stylized as ever, every price in plain points, no instrument named. A strong leg is under way, and for once both traders are long in it, and both are correct. What separates them is not the entry. It is what they do with a winner while it is still winning.

Watch the leg while it behaves. It travels the way a healthy move travels: clean swings, each high above the last, each pullback shallow and quickly reclaimed, delivery away from every pause efficient and unlabored. The candles are full-bodied and one-directional. A leg that moves like this is telling you, in the only grammar the market owns, that it intends to continue, and both traders are being paid to believe it. Here, so far, there is no argument between them.

The first trader does what winning invites. He falls in love. The position is green and growing, and the growth persuades him that the growth is owed. He stops examining the move and starts admiring it. He has a stop somewhere below, but the profit has made it abstract, and as the leg climbs he does the two things a winner most reliably seduces a man into doing. He trails his stop up on hope rather than on structure, tucking it closer each time so that he need never give much back, and he inflates the fantasy of where the move must reach. His examination has run backward again, exactly as it did when he was losing, only now the verdict he defends is a pleasant one. He is no longer trading the leg. He is trading his opinion of it.

The second trader did something duller at the very start. She framed the trade before she took it, and the frame named, in writing, the price that would say the idea was wrong and the gates along the route where she would take her tolls. So as the leg travels she harvests it in pieces. At each gate the structure projects she brings a portion off, banks it, and arms it against whatever comes next. Her invalidation does not move. It sits where she placed it, beneath the structure that authored the leg, the one price on her chart she has forbidden herself to touch. She is not trying to catch the exact top. She has traded that ambition for something worth more: a position already paid for, and an eye left free to watch.

Then the leg stops behaving like itself, and this is the whole of the reading. Nothing breaks. No level gives way, no line is crossed, and the untrained eye, the first trader's eye, sees only another higher high and better prices still. But the character has changed, and the character is what the tenth truth told you to keep in writing. The swings have shrunk. The pushes that were clean are now overlapping and labored, bought expensively, each giving back most of what it made. The full-bodied candles have become small and two-directional, wicks at both ends, the print of a market arguing with itself where lately it simply traveled. A leg that has stopped moving like itself has, more often than not, changed hands. Character breaks first. Structure breaks last.

The second trader is not surprised, because she was reading the behavior and not merely the price. The move no longer resembles the one she was paid to hold, so she takes the remainder off at the structure while it is still there to be sold into, and steps aside with the campaign banked. The first trader sees the same candles and reads them as a pause, a gathering, a base for the next push. He holds, because holding has worked all day, and because letting go would mean admitting the top was already in. His trailed stop, set on hope, is either too close and takes him out on the first honest pullback for a fraction of what the leg offered, or too far and waits patiently to give back a fortune.

Then it turns, as a move whose character has gone will turn. The reversal is quick, because the buyers who authored the leg have already left, and it runs down through the labored little swings, through the first trader's hope, and takes back most of what the morning gave him. He closes at last, well below the top he was so sure of, holding a profit a fraction of the one he sat on at the high, and a story about how the market let him down. The ledger tells it without mercy. Both traders read the same leg. One harvested it at the gates and left the moment it stopped being itself. The other rode it up on structure and back down on hope, and paid the difference in full.

This is the tax the market collects on attachment, and it is the most voluntary tax there is. The entry was never the hard part here; both had it. The discipline was in the holding: to take the tolls that were framed, to watch the character rather than the price, and to let a winner go the instant it stops behaving like a winner. Profit protected is the only profit there is. Everything else is a loan the market will call, with interest, on the day the leg stops behaving like itself.

The gates this reading tested are the Sequence's last, and they decide not whether you get in but what you keep. The harvest, taken in pieces at the gates the structure projected. The invalidation, placed once beneath the move's author and never moved again. And the character, the eye the tenth and eleventh truths trained, which reads a winner while it is still winning and lets it go the moment it stops behaving like one. The Sequence earns the position. Only these keep it. That is where these readings have been walking you from the first morning.

CHAPTER 12

PSYCHOLOGY

The Deep End

The industry preaches that trading is mostly psychology, and then sells psychology as though it could be installed. It cannot. Confidence, patience, and discipline are not inputs a trader brings to the work; they are outputs the work produces when it is correctly ordered. Bad order makes bad psychology. Losses that cannot be explained manufacture fear; wins that cannot be repeated manufacture gamblers. Build the foundation in its sequence, and the mind the gurus keep promising will build itself.

TRANSGRESSION OF THE TRUTH

SURVEY HOW THE PERFORMING world actually builds its performers, because the pattern is so uniform that its single exception will be visible from orbit. Aviation takes a person who dreams of flight and puts them in a simulator, then beside an instructor, then solo in clear weather over empty country, then instrument-rated, then type-rated, hour upon logged hour, each new exposure unlocked by demonstrated competence at the last. Surgery takes its aspirants through years of watching, then retracting, then closing, then operating under eyes, before a life is ever theirs alone. Chess grades its children into rating bands where novices play novices and rise one plateau at a time. Sport, the purest case, builds by age group and division: development squads, junior circuits, graduated opposition, the right competition at the right time, because every coach alive knows that a champion is manufactured by a long ladder of contests each chosen to stretch and none chosen to drown. No coach on earth throws a promising swimmer into an Olympic final and instructs them to win gold and grow from the experience. The coach who tried would be dismissed before the water settled, and the sport would call it what it is: the destruction of an athlete.

Now regard trading, the one performance arena on the planet that sells the deep end as the entry point. A novice opens an account in an afternoon, and by evening is competing, with real leverage and the rent money, in the same pool as the fastest and best-capitalized competitors our species has produced, in the single most adversarial environment ever constructed. There is no ladder. There is no age group. There is no instructor with a hand on the controls, no rating band protecting the six-hundred-rated player from the grandmaster, no junior circuit; there is the open ocean on day one, and a cheerful login screen where the pool fence ought to be. Every other discipline rations exposure to match development, because exposure beyond development does not teach, it wounds. Trading inverts the entire accumulated wisdom of human performance, hands the beginner its hardest problem first, and then, when the predictable happens, delivers the industry's unanimous diagnosis: the problem, you see, was the novice's mindset.

Watch what the deep end actually manufactures, because the mechanism is precise. The novice loses, as he must, and the loss is illegible: he cannot know which of a hundred uncontrolled variables killed him, the entry, the hour, the size, the instrument, the regime, the spread, or nothing at all, mere variance. An illegible loss teaches exactly one thing: fear without an address. Then he wins occasionally, and the win is equally illegible, which is worse: it teaches that outcomes are magic, unmoored from anything he did, and magic is the operating system of the gambler. Losses without levers produce what the laboratory calls learned helplessness and what the trading forum calls tilt, revenge, paralysis, the yips: an organism punished on no schedule it can decode will first rage, then flail, then quit or break. Read the catalogue of trading's famous demons honestly and one thing becomes clear: these are not causes of failure. They are symptoms of illegibility. Bad psychology is not why the deep end defeats the novice. Bad psychology is what the deep end manufactures out of him.

And the wound compounds, because the first truth's law of skill formation works in the deep end too, in reverse. A skill is assembled from repetitions, and the drowning man is repeating something every single day: improvised entries, unframed exits, punishment without pattern, and above all the emotional sequence of hope, spike, and regret. Ten thousand disordered repetitions do not leave a person where he started; they build expertise in disorder, panic practiced into fluency, flinch drilled into reflex. This is why the veteran of five losing years is often harder to develop than the untouched beginner, and every real coach knows the phenomenon: the self-taught athlete arrives not as a blank page but as a page of ingrained errors that must be unlearned at double cost. The deep end is not a harsh school. It is a school with a curriculum, and the curriculum is the destruction of exactly the faculties the work requires.

And then, in the transgression's final insult, the industry sells the cure for the wound it inflicted. Be disciplined, says the course. Master your emotions, says the book. Journal your feelings, breathe before the open, visualize the trader you wish to become: an entire economy of mindset, marketed to people still in the water, still without a single lever they can name, still incapable, through no fault of character, of knowing why any given trade won or lost. None of it is false. All of it is out of order. You cannot meditate your way out of an environment that outclasses your development; you cannot affirm a foundation into existence; and a man drowning in the deep end does not have a mindset problem. He has a location problem, and the first truth of this book applies to careers exactly as it applied to charts: nothing becomes reliable until it is placed in the right order.

INTERPRETATION

LOCATE THE INVERSION PRECISELY, because this chapter does not say what a careless reader will take it to say. Psychology matters in trading enormously; the industry's observation is correct, and the great performance coaches would co-sign it. What is backwards is the causality. Champion psychology is not an ingredient that produces champion performance; it is a residue that ordered development leaves behind. The athlete who wins legibly, on a ladder, at the right grade, banks evidence: I did the work, the work produced this, I know which lever produced which result. Stack years of that and you get what the crowd calls temperament: the calm that is actually a ledger. The athlete who loses continually, illegibly, out of his grade, banks the opposite evidence and becomes the opposite thing. Winning builds winners and losing drills losing, not as slogans but as the compounding of legible outcomes into identity, and the direction of the whole cascade runs from order to psyche. The industry sells the residue and skips the development. It has the tail wagging the champion.

The coach's version of mindset work proves the point rather than contradicting it, because coaches do train the mind, constantly, and always in the same position: on top of competence, never in place of it. The confidence a coach installs before a final is evidentiary: you have made this jump ten thousand times in training, your splits this season are the proof, trust the preparation. Every sentence points at a ledger. What affirmation could compete with evidence, and what evidence could a novice trader's affirmations point at? The mind is not built by talking to it. It is built by giving it something true to stand on, and the truths of this book, it turns out, were the something.

OBSERVANCE OF THE TRUTH

IN BUDAPEST IN THE 1960s, an educational psychologist named László Polgár spent years in the biographies of the world's acknowledged geniuses, looking for the common inheritance, and concluded that there wasn't one: what the geniuses shared was not blood but circumstance, early immersion, structured work, and the right challenges at the right time. Geniuses, he wrote, are made, not born, and the academy laughed at him. His response has no parallel in the history of stubbornness: he decided to run the experiment on his own unborn children, and he courted his future wife, a schoolteacher named Klara, partly by correspondence outlining the project. The couple chose chess as the laboratory, not out of family passion but for the coldest of experimental reasons: chess keeps score. Progress in chess is objective, measurable, and public, a rating instead of an opinion. Then they had three daughters, and raised them on the plan.

The Polgár home was a development machine of exactly the kind the deep end never provides. The girls were educated at home, and chess was structured into the day with thousands of volumes and a vast handbuilt card index of positions and games: the material graded, the study ordered, the work daily and legible. And the competition was rationed with a coach's precision: tournaments chosen to stretch, never to drown, each opponent a size too big and no more, so that losses arrived in analyzable quantities and wins arrived earned. The results embarrassed every critic the project had. Zsuzsa, the eldest, became the first woman to earn the grandmaster title through standard tournament play. Zsófia, at fourteen, produced the tournament of legend in Rome, sweeping a field of masters at a performance level almost no player of any age has matched. And Judit, the youngest, refused the shelter of women's events entirely, played the open field her whole career, took the grandmaster title at fifteen years and four months, younger than Fischer, and stood for decades as the strongest female chess player in history, a fixture of the world's top ten who defeated Kasparov, Karpov, and nearly every world champion of her era.

Now attend to the detail that makes this the observance of this chapter and not merely of ambition: what the chess world marveled at, almost more than the sisters' play, was their temperament. Judit at fifteen sat across from world champions without a visible nerve; losses that would have unspooled seasoned grandmasters were absorbed, analyzed, and converted; the composure was so complete that commentators reached for words like fearless and unnatural. It was neither. It was manufactured, and not by a single hour of what the trading industry would recognize as mindset work. It was the residue of tens of thousands of legible outcomes: every loss returned to the card index and dissected until it surrendered its lever, every win traceable to preparation the family could point to, every tournament graded to development so that the evidence always meant something. Fearlessness against Kasparov was not courage summoned on the day. It was a ledger, decades deep, being consulted. And the daughters, asked as adults about the strange engineered childhood, defended it as a happy one, which completes the experiment: the development plan did not merely produce champions. It produced champions who owned the plan.

INTERPRETATION

THE EXPERIMENT ISOLATES THE variable with a cleanness no laboratory could improve. Three sisters, three visibly different personalities, one development system, three champions: temperament was not the input. And the deep-end industry runs the counter-experiment every day at global scale: every temperament humanity offers, no system at all, and one overwhelming result. If psychology were the ingredient, the Polgár range of temperaments should have produced a range of outcomes, and trading's infinite range of temperaments should occasionally produce accidental masses of champions. Neither happens. The system is the signal; the temperament is noise around it, and the noise converges toward confidence wherever the system makes outcomes legible, and toward wreckage wherever it does not.

The trader's difficulty, and it is real, is that no one will run the Polgár household for you: you are the coach and the athlete, the parent and the prodigy, in one skull, which is the same crowded arrangement that ruined Livermore until you remember that this book spent eleven chapters building the separation. The curriculum is the truths. The card index is the ledger and the audit. The graded tournaments are the ladder of exposure this chapter will lay out in a moment. Self-coached does not mean uncoached; it means the development plan must be written down, like everything else in this book, where the athlete cannot lose it and the coach cannot soften it. What the Polgárs prove is that the writing works: that psychology yields to architecture, in children and therefore certainly in adults, and that the residue called champion temperament will condense on any career conducted in the right order.

KEYS TO THE TRUTH

STATE THE THEOREM. NOTICE it only needs saying once, because everything after it is corollary: right technicals build right psychology, and the reverse path does not exist. The reason is structural, not motivational. The mind cannot durably hold what evidence contradicts. Confidence affirmed in the mirror dies at the first drawdown. The drawdown is evidence, and the affirmation was decoration. But confidence that is a memory of legible wins survives drawdowns easily. The drawdown and the confidence are entries in the same honest ledger. The ledger has seen this weather before. Patience installed as a resolution lasts until the first missed train. Patience that is knowledge is different. It is the third truth's certainty that there is always another train, and the tenth's knowledge of when it tends to arrive. That is not patience at all in the willpower sense. It is simply what a person with that information does. Every virtue the industry sells is downstream of information ordered correctly. That is why no trader was ever therapized into consistency, and thousands have been sequenced into it.

Understand tilt, the industry's great demon, as this book understands it. Watch it shrink from character flaw to engineering defect. The human brain is a lever-finding machine. It exists to connect action to outcome. Feed it outcomes with no findable levers and it does one of two things, both catastrophic in markets. It invents levers, and you get superstition: the lucky session, the cursed instrument, the guru's secret hour, Kircher returned as self-help. Or it concludes no levers exist. Then you get the collapse the laboratory calls helplessness and the floor calls the yips. Rage, the acute form, is the organism's ancient response to unearned punishment: strike back at the thing that hurt you outside the rules. But the framed trader is never unearnedly punished. His losses have addresses, named in advance. His punishments arrive by appointment: at the death line, at premise-impeachment, at the expiry. Each one is legible. Each one is convertible into a lever by that evening's autopsy. Tilt cannot metabolize a loss that was scheduled. The demon is not slain by breathing exercises. It is starved by legibility.

Now the reveal this chapter has been building toward. The attentive reader has already felt it. The technical curriculum of this book was the psychological curriculum all along. Take the industry's catalog of mental demons and hold it against the truths. Overwhelm, the firehose of the screen, died in the first truth. A fixed sequence is the end of drowning in information. Self-deception died in the second. Has and has not leave no room for the stories traders tell themselves. The fear of missing out died across the third and fourth. The trader who knows the market always returns to value, and that a train missed is only a station kept, has nothing to chase. The boredom trade died in the fifth, on a clock that names the empty hours. Prediction anxiety died in the sixth, when the job became reading the present instead of guessing the future. Performance panic died in the seventh, where the frame decides everything before the fire begins. Size-fear died in the eighth, where size became a quotient. The terror of loss died in the ninth, where every loss was budgeted before birth. Surprise died in the tenth, demoted to diagnosis. Self-worth detached from outcomes in the eleventh, when identity moved its residence from the trade to the series. Twelve chapters of technique. Behind them, invisible, a complete course of therapy that never once mentioned feelings. That is not a coincidence. That is the causality running in its true direction.

The ladder, then, since you must build your own. Exposure is rationed to development, the coach's periodization translated to the screen. First, observation with the sequence. Read sessions in the first truth's order, no capital at risk. Continue until the verdicts of the sixth truth are called correctly in real time and the calls are logged. Then simulation, not as a toy but as the flight simulator it is. Fly full frames, tolls, graves and audits. Continue until the ledger shows the process operating, not just the ideas appearing. Then minimum size, the smallest real unit the instrument allows. Simulation cannot teach what a heartbeat does to a frame. This rung exists precisely to make that lesson cheap. Then scale, in steps. Each promotion is purchased with the only currency the coach accepts:

blocks of framed trades at the current rung with breach rates near zero and leakage tagged and falling. Not profit. Breach rates. Profit at a given rung is partly weather. Obedience is entirely climate. And promotion on weather is how the deep end sneaks back into a laddered career. The impatient will call this slow. It is the fastest path that exists. It is the only one where the trader who arrives at size still exists to use it.

One definition deserves its full weight here, because it names both halves and the industry audits only one. Good psychology comes from understanding why you win and why you lose. The losses get the autopsies. Almost nobody dissects a win. And undissected wins are where gamblers incubate inside otherwise developing traders. For every winner in the ledger, the audit asks the same questions it asks of the dead. Was the claim framed? Did the entry come at the station on signature? Was the harvest taken at the surveyed gates? Or did this profit arrive despite the process, weather mislabeled as skill? A win that survives that examination is a lever confirmed, and confidence banks it. A win that fails it is tagged like any other leakage. Profitable leakage is the most dangerous substance in the building. The Polgár card index did not only hold the losses. Mastery is symmetrical bookkeeping. The trader who can explain his wins is the only one entitled to trust them.

Guard especially against the hazard nobody warns beginners about, because it photographs so well: the large early win. The novice who loses small and legibly in his first season is being developed. The novice who wins big and illegibly is being damaged, often permanently. The win installs the gambler's operating system with cash. It certifies magic as method. He will spend years and fortunes trying to reproduce an outcome that had no levers. The industry will sell him psychology when what he owns is a corrupted bootloader. If early fortune strikes you, treat it as the process treats any unframed outcome. Bank it. Tag it as weather. Return to the rung you were actually on. The ledger knows the difference between what you earned and what you caught. Make sure you agree with the ledger.

Hear the difference in a training diary. The texture of legibility is unmistakable. The deep-end trader's journal, week one: Lost again, don't know what happened, market turned right where I entered like it saw me, felt stupid, revenge traded the news, worse. Every sentence is a symptom:

no levers, invented agency, punishment without address, the spiral. Now the same trader, a year into the order. Same market, same temperament. He writes: Breached sequence at step three, read the trigger before the environment, tagged leakage, lever is the pre-session checklist, size unaffected, else-nothing respected rest of day. Not a feeling in it. Yet it is the psychologically healthier document by any measure a clinician could name. Agency located, punishment explained, improvement specified, identity intact. Nobody taught that trader mindset. Somebody taught him order, and the mindset condensed on it like dew.

There is a simple field test for whether the development has taken. It costs one question: ask the trader why he makes money. The undeveloped answer is a result: I'm up this quarter, the account has grown, it's been working. The developed answer is a mechanism, spoken in levers. I make money because I examine the market in a fixed order. I engage only at surveyed locations, at a discount or premium to value, at hours that produce my structures. My claims are framed in advance, my losses budgeted at structural graves, my tolls collected at the stations. And my breach rate is the number I manage. The first answer describes weather and will change with it. The second describes a machine. Its owner's confidence is not a mood that the next drawdown can repossess. It is a description of equipment he can point to, part by part. When your answer to the question becomes boring, mechanical, and exact, the psychology the industry keeps selling has quietly become something you own.

Concede, finally, what remains. The honest version of this chapter is stronger than the triumphant one. Order does not abolish the person. Sleep, health, the pressures of a life outside the screen, the genuine article of temperament, grief and ego and fear in their raw forms: these are real. They trade with you every day. No sequence dissolves them. The claim of this chapter was never that psychology is nothing. It is that psychology is last, the residue examined after order has absorbed everything order can absorb. So run the diagnostic in its proper sequence, like everything else you now own. When results bleed, exhaust the procedural explanation first: the breach rates, the leakage, the ladder rung, the legibility of the losses. Only when the process is demonstrably clean and the bleeding continues does the remainder earn the name psychological. That remainder deserves direct work, human work, sometimes professional work. In practice the remainder is small. In practice, almost everything that presents at the trading desk as a broken person is a broken order, wearing feelings. The repair sequence this book has taught you never changes: fix the order first.

IMAGE

The Deep End. Watch where champions are made: in lanes, in lengths, in drills, in races each chosen one size too big and none chosen to drown, a childhood of graded water. The man thrown into the deep end is also getting exposure, the brochure is technically correct, and what he is learning, lungs full of chlorine, is panic, and panic practiced daily becomes expertise like anything else. The water is the same water in both pools. The difference is the order in which it is met, and no one was ever coached to gold from the bottom of the pool.

AUTHORITY

"We are what we repeatedly do. Excellence, then, is not an act, but a habit."
— Will Durant, summarizing Aristotle, The Story of Philosophy, 1926

REVERSAL

THE LADDER HAS A corruption of its own: the climber who never leaves it. Graduated exposure decays, in the fearful, into perpetual preparation: the eternal simulator pilot, the trader on minimum size in his fourth year, one more block of trades, one more course, one more refinement before the water above the knee. Understand what he has actually built, because it is subtler than cowardice: he has discovered that the development plan, pursued forever, is the one place in trading where you cannot be proven wrong, and he has turned the coach's ladder into the perfectionist's shut frame from the seventh truth, a hiding place with excellent paperwork. Development means graduation; the grades exist to be left. The coach who never enters his athlete in the meet is not protecting her. He is consuming her career, and the self-coached trader can commit that crime against himself with no one to notice for years.

And the chapter's own thesis over-corrects into a final trap: psychology-denial, the trader who has learned that feelings are usually symptoms and concludes they are never signal. His process is clean, his breach rates are zero, his ledger bleeds anyway, and he responds by auditing the process again, and again, because looking there is more comfortable than looking anywhere else: procedure as the last place to hide from the person. The rule of this book cuts both ways and must be allowed to: exhaust the procedural explanation first, and then honor what remains. When the order is demonstrably clean and the damage continues, the remainder is real, it is human, and it does not yield to one more audit. There is no shame in the remainder. There is only the same discipline that governed everything else: the correct diagnosis, in the correct sequence, and the humility to accept what the ledger, that most patient of coaches, has been trying to say.

The twelve truths now stand complete: six that taught you to see, three that taught you to act, and three that taught you to continue, with this last revealing what the whole structure was quietly building while you thought it was building trades. One thing remains, and it is short: to look at the twelve as a single object, once, before the book lets you go.

A FIFTH READING

THE TRADE THAT DIED ON SCHEDULE

This last reading is the one the others earned. Four times you have watched the sequence win. Watch what it does on the morning it loses, because that morning is not an exception to the doctrine. It is the doctrine.

WATCH THE TWO TRADERS one final time. The same market, the same session, and for once the same conclusion: both are short, from the same shelf, within minutes of each other. The scene is deliberately ordinary. A campaign has carried price down for days, paused, and lifted into a zone of prior supply. The first trader arrives by feel. The move looks tired, the level looks heavy, and heavy is a word he could not define under oath. He sells because it has gone up enough. The second trader arrives by the gates. The governing read is markdown. The location is surveyed, an origin overhead, stated in exact prices. The lift into it has the shape of an errand, not a change of heart. At the sub-location the close prints where it must print, and she takes the entry on the verdict, never on the hope of one. Beneath the shelf that authored her claim she fixes the grave, at the price that unsays it, and writes the whole of it down before the market can answer: three exact prices, an expiry, an else-nothing. Two shorts. A stranger watching both screens would swear they hold the same trade. You know better by now.

Overnight the market files its objection. A report neither trader could have read in advance lands before the open, and the tape that follows does not argue: the shelf is taken back, the origin absorbed, the swing that authored the decline buried under acceptance. This is not noise against a good claim. It is the map impeached, the tenth truth arriving on the clock it always keeps. Price walks up through her stated price and her position is gone, one order, no negotiation, the loss the frame had budgeted on the day it was written. She reads the impeachment and re-surveys. The premise did not fail quietly somewhere inside her conviction. It failed publicly, at a price, and the price had been named in advance. That is all a clean death is: the else-nothing verdict, delivered late.

The first trader is also underwater, and here his morning turns lucky, which is the worst thing that can happen to him. He has no grave, so nothing forces his hand. He endures, doubles once because it had to turn, and the market, owing him nothing, turns. The report is walked back by noon, the move fails, and price sags to his entry and beyond. He covers for a profit and a story. By any audit the book has taught, the win cannot survive examination. No claim, no location, no signature, no stated death. Profit arrived despite the process, weather mislabeled as skill. He banks the money and, far more expensively, the lesson: that holding saved him. He will spend the rest of his career paying that lesson back.

Run the morning a hundred times and the ledgers separate on schedule. Her hundred mornings contain that loss again and again, and it never grows. It is the premium the frame pays for certainty about the one thing the market guarantees, which is the surprise. His hundred mornings contain the rescue less and less, and the one morning it does not come takes back every coin the habit ever lent him, with interest. She was not wrong that morning. She was early to be right about the only thing worth being right about: that no reading, however ordered, outranks the tape's verdict on it. The sequence did not fail her. It performed its final duty, the one it was built for first. It made the cost of being wrong small, known, and paid in advance.

Note what the loss did not touch. Not the survey, which was accurate until the world changed. Not the signature, which was real when it printed. Not her. The account is smaller by one budgeted premium and the process is intact, which means the account is intact where it matters, in its ability to run tomorrow. That is the whole of it. The doctrine never promised you the morning. It promised you the series, and the series is where the two traders part for good: one of them is paid for his worst habit, and one of them has just been billed, precisely, for her best one.

CODA

THE ESSENTIAL TRUTH

RETURN, ONE LAST TIME, to the morning this book opened on. Napoleon at Waterloo lacked nothing that talent can supply. He had the finest military mind of his age, veterans who worshiped him, and information as good as his enemy's. What he lacked was buried in no textbook and visible on no map: an order for examining what he knew that could exist outside his own weather, a sequence that worked when he was tired, a clock he had consented to obey, a machine that did not require him to be magnificent that particular day. And across the field stood the future in embryo: within two generations, the unglamorous Prussian system of ordered examination would make average men collectively unbeatable and place every army on earth in its debt. Nobody ever managed to copy the Emperor. Everybody copied the sequence. That asymmetry is the essential truth of this book, and every chapter has been one facet of it turned to the light.

Here is the whole architecture, named once as a single object. Examine the market in a fixed sequence, so that what you see is perception and not preconception. Anchor every judgment to markers two observers could not dispute, in the only tense the market speaks: has, and has not. Know where price stands on its journey, from what origin toward what destination, because between stations you are guessing and at them you are reading. Measure every position against value, the current range within its governing range, so that each entry is one of two honest acts: buying discount or selling premium. Give every observation its key time, for nothing in the market means anything except at its time. Read the language, structure's verdicts at appointed places, and never finish the market's sentences for it. Then act like a professional and not a prophet: frame the claim before the trial, three exact prices and the evidence that defeats it; derive every number from the ground, never from your needs; place the grave where the premise dies and let no one, least of all you, move it. And then continue: trust the reflection but never bill for it; run the machine that harvests journeys and pays you at every gate; and understand that the machine's final product, assembled silently across years of legible outcomes, is you. The same sequence, stated operationally and step by step, stands as an appendix at the close of this book: one page, meant to be copied and hung where you trade.

Notice what is absent from that paragraph. There is no prediction in it anywhere. At no step were you asked to know the future, and this is the discovery that separates the consistent from the crowd: the entire apparatus of professional trading can be assembled without a single act of prophecy. The crowd believes the successful trader knows something about tomorrow. He does not. He knows something about procedure: that the same information, examined in the same order, through markers that cannot be argued with, at locations and hours where answers mean something, framed so that being wrong is cheap and being right is harvested, produces a result that prophecy has never once produced for anyone: consistency. The market shows every participant the same picture. It always has. The difference was never in the picture.

It follows, and it must be said plainly once, that the search most traders are on is misdirected at its root. The missing thing is not an indicator, and it is not a secret, and it is not the mindset the industry bottles, and it is not more information, of which you already had more than the men who built fortunes with a ticker tape. The missing thing was always sequence: the order in which the ordinary is examined. That is a hard sale in a business that markets lightning, because sequence is unglamorous, learnable, and free, and nothing free and learnable feels like it could be the answer. The Prussians heard the same objection from every officer who preferred genius. The answer outlasted all of them.

What this book has given you is the sequence and its truths; what it has deliberately not given you is your instrument's particulars, your timeframe's tempos, the specific stations and signatures of the markets you trade, the calibrations that turn a constitution into a working machine. Those are craft, they are learnable too, and they belong to the work that comes after a book: the ten thousand ordered repetitions, the card index that only you can build, and, for those who want the development plan run at the shoulder rather than alone, the more particular teaching that lives outside these pages. The truths tell you what must be done and in what order. Where exactly, on your chart, at your size, is the apprenticeship this book was written to make possible.

So end where the first truth began, because the ring was always going to close here. A trader stands before a screen that shows them what it shows everyone: the same prices, the same hours, the same journeys assembling and completing. Everything now depends, as everything always depended, on the order in which they meet it: sequence before sight, markers before belief, place before action, value before price, the hour before the act, reading before responding, the frame before the trial, the survey before the numbers, the grave before the entry, the reflection before the expectation, the machine before the outcome, and the order, all of it, before the trader, because the order is what builds them. The market will not remember your name, and it does not need to. It keeps only one ledger, and it has kept it since the first two humans disagreed about the price of grain: the patient record of who examined the world in sequence, and who examined it in whatever order their hunger chose. Nothing becomes reliable until it is placed in the right order. Not even you.

APPENDIX

THE SEQUENCE, STATED

THE FIRST TRUTH MADE a promise. The order of examination would come in time. It has been assembling through every chapter since, and here it stands as one object, in the author's own working order, stated operationally. It is printed on one page for a reason. Copy it, and hang it where you trade.

EACH GATE OPENS ONLY ONTO THE NEXT

1. Governing Cycle & Model
2. Location
3. Lower Timeframe Cycle Position
4. Value
5. Time
6. Measure Market Structure
7. Frame
8. Signature · Perfect Pricing
9. Invalidation

This is the Order, stated as steps: the Sequence. Each gate opens only onto the next.

I. GOVERNING CYCLE & MODEL

Fix the position in the higher-timeframe cycle: accumulation, advance, re-accumulation, or distribution. The governing cycle decides which claims may be filed at all, and its model is the one the day will obey.

II. LOCATION

Locate price on the map. What origin authored the current journey, and what destination does the route imply? Station or transit, in exact prices.

III. LOWER TIMEFRAME CYCLE POSITION

Fix the lower-timeframe cycle within the governing one: the local campaign inside the greater, the telescope turned one magnification in.

IV. VALUE

Read the value position. Discount or premium, inside the discount or premium of the governing range. Dear governs cheap, always.

V. TIME

Consult the clock. Session, window, and the participation due or departing. Nothing means anything except at its time.

VI. MEASURE MARKET STRUCTURE

Measure the market through the phases of its cycle: accumulation, the purge that clears one side of the book, the shift that authors the move. Confirm what price has held, what it has swept, and which candle signed the turn you propose to trust. Read the structure in the only tense the market speaks: has, and has not.

VII. FRAME

Frame the claim: three exact prices, an expiry, and an else-nothing, written where it cannot be unwritten. Then measure everything it asserts, projections converging on the objective and the envelope of ordinary hostility around the entry. Size is the quotient and nothing else.

VIII. SIGNATURE · PERFECT PRICING

The language's verdict at the appointed place. At surveyed sub-locations, demand the purest of them: the perfect close at the exact price. The entry is taken on it, never on the hope of one. Its appearance is never described in these pages; it is shown. Study the figures, and the Readings, until you would know it on sight.

IX. INVALIDATION

Place the grave beneath the accumulation that authored the move, beyond the noise, at the price that unsays the claim. Then surrender the right to move it anywhere but forward.

This is not the only workable sequence. But any workable sequence must gate in this direction. Context before detail, conditions before conclusions, environment before entry. The claim before the trial, the grave before the entry, the series before the self. This one is the author's, built and paid for over the years this book distills. Build yours in its image, examine your market through it in the same order every time, and treat any breach of it as an error regardless of the outcome of the trade. Nothing becomes reliable until it is placed in the right order.

THE COMPANION

essentialtruthsoftrading.com/seqorder

The Sequence of this book, walked live, gate by gate.

AFTERWORD

ON WHAT COMES AFTER

A BOOK CAN GIVE you the truths, and this one has given you everything I know how to put on paper: the sequence, the eye, the map, the appraisal, the clock, the language, the frame, the survey, the grave, the reflection, the machine, and the person the machine builds. What no book can give you is the apprenticeship: the ten thousand ordered repetitions, the card index that only your own markets can fill, the calibrations of your instrument, your timeframe, your session, your size. That work is where every reader of every trading book either becomes a trader or becomes a collector of trading books, and the difference, as always, is not information. It is whether the repetitions are done, in order, with the outcomes made legible and the record kept honestly.

Some readers will build that apprenticeship alone, with this book's appendix hung where they trade, and it can be done that way; the pilot's river can be learned from the wheelhouse. For those who choose to go further, the same work continues at essentialtruthsoftrading.com, in the same order and under the same truths: the where to this book's what, the specific locations, signatures, and calibrations that these pages deliberately hold at the level of principle. The truths came first, and they are yours now either way.

A GLOSSARY OF TERMS

The book's working vocabulary, defined as the chapters use it.

GOVERNING CYCLE · The higher-timeframe cycle that decides which trades may be taken at all: accumulation, advance, re-accumulation, or distribution. Its model is the one the day will obey.

MODEL · The market-maker template of a cycle, from which each phase, gap, and wick is read as a location.

LOCATION · A place on the map where price answers questions, an origin or a destination, stated in exact prices rather than zones.

SUB-LOCATION · A precise level within a location, where the perfect close at the exact price is demanded.

VALUE · The reference from which movement is measured; price read as discount or premium within the governing range.

THE FIFTY · The midpoint of a range, the line between discount and premium.

TIME · The session, window, and moment at which a location is due to matter. Nothing means anything except at its time.

LANGUAGE · The market's continuous report of structure, location, value, and time; read, never predicted.

FRAME · The written claim of a trade: three exact prices, an expiry, and an else-nothing, fixed before the market can answer.

MEASUREMENT · The proof that a location is real, expressed as projections and the quotient that becomes size.

PERFECT PRICING · The market's cleanest verdict at an exact price: a close that answers the level rather than merely touches it. The signature demanded at a sub-location before an entry is taken. Described nowhere; shown in the figures.

SIGNATURE · The verdict the market's language delivers at the appointed place, candle by candle.

INVALIDATION · The price at which the premise is unsaid; the stop placed where price should not trade if the premise holds.

ACCUMULATION · DISTRIBUTION · RE-DISTRIBUTION · Position built at a low; position unloaded at a high; distribution resumed at a lower high.

SWEEP · The clearing of one side of the book, the run that takes stops before the true move.

SEQUENCE · The nine gates in fixed order, each opening only onto the next; the Order stated as steps.

KEY TIME · The specific time assigned to an observation, without which it carries no verdict.

ATTRIBUTIONS, NOTES AND SOURCES

A DEBT OWED PLAINLY, and first. The technical apparatus these pages arrange is not original to me, and the precision of it least of all. The fair value gap and the optimal trade entry, the market maker's accumulation and distribution, the signature of a perfect price and the time windows in which it prints: for that body of teaching I am indebted above all to Michael J. Huddleston, known to many as the Inner Circle Trader, whose work shaped the specific mechanics on which the later chapters draw, and their precision most of all. Behind him stands Richard Wyckoff, whose schematics of accumulation and distribution remain the grammar of market structure a century on. What this book claims as its own is not the pieces but their order: the truths that govern them, and the sequence that puts them to work. The precision is inspired by theirs; the arrangement, and any fault in it, is mine.

On the industry's casualty rate: European regulators require brokers of leveraged retail products to publish the percentage of client accounts that lose money; the disclosed figures have typically run between seventy and eighty-nine percent. The academic record concurs: see Barber and Odean, "Trading Is Hazardous to Your Wealth" (Journal of Finance, 2000), and Barber, Lee, Liu and Odean's studies of Taiwanese day traders, which found that only a small percentage traded profitably after costs over the long run.

The historical accounts in this book are told from the standard published sources, including: David McCullough, The Path Between the Seas (Panama); Atul Gawande, The Checklist Manifesto, and the U.S. Air Force's public accounts of the Model 299; the Royal Society's Notes and Records paper on Newton's South Sea transactions (2019), which supplied the corrected figures used in Chapter 2; Edwin Lefèvre, Reminiscences of a Stock Operator (1923), and Livermore's own How to Trade in Stocks (1940); Mark Twain, Life on the Mississippi (1883); Benjamin Graham, The Intelligent Investor, chapter 8; the scholarly record of Rush v. Cobbett (1799), including the same-day coincidence with Washington's death noted in Chapter 7; and the standard accounts of the Dojima rice market, the Polgár family, the 1913 Monte Carlo run, the ERM crisis of 1992, and the collapse of Barings. Where a detail rests on tradition rather than record, the text says so where it stands. Quotations are verbatim from their stated sources; the small number that history attributes rather than records are marked attributed in place.

ABOUT THE AUTHOR

THE AUTHOR HAS WATCHED the markets daily for two decades, a discipline woven through the whole of his life and career. His earlier careers run wider than most: the law, practiced at the sharp end; elite sport, first as a competitor and then as a coach; and business, where he has founded and built companies, led an investment firm, and patented inventions along the way. A working life spent, one way or another, in rooms where sequence decides outcomes, and where he learned the habit this book teaches: that the plan is written in the cool hour, and the fire does not get a vote. He writes under a pen name, for professional reasons, and is content for the book to be judged by its only relevant credential: whether the sequence holds when you test it.

www.ingramcontent.com/pod-product-compliance
Lightning Source LLC
LaVergne TN
LVHW020234210926
848481LV00016B/1948
* 9 7 8 1 7 6 4 8 1 4 5 0 8 *